PERGAMON INTERNATIONAL LIBRARY
of Science, Technology, Engineering and Social Studies
the 1000-volume original paperback library in aid of education
industrial training and the enjoyment of leisure

2—

Social Work Research
and the
Analysis of Social Data

D0162347

SOCIAL WORK DIVISION

General Editor: JEAN P. NURSTEN

Other Books in this Series

Social Work Research
and the
Analysis of Social Data

A. E. PHILIP
Principal Clinical Psychologist, Banguor Village Hospital,
Broxburn, West Lothian

J. W. McCULLOCH
Director of Social Work Research Unit, School of Applied
Social Studies, University of Bradford

and

N. J. SMITH
Member of Social Work Research Unit, School of Applied
Social Studies, University of Bradford

PERGAMON PRESS
OXFORD · NEW YORK · TORONTO
SYDNEY · BRAUNSCHWEIG

U. K.	Pergamon Press Ltd., Headington Hill Hall, Oxford, England
U. S. A.	Pergamon Press Inc., Maxwell House, Fairview Park, Elmsford, New York 10523, U.S.A.
CANADA	Pergamon of Canada Ltd., 207 Queen's Quay West, Toronto 1, Canada
AUSTRALIA	Pergamon Press (Aust.) Pty. Ltd., 19a Boundary Street, Rushcutters Bay, N.S.W. 2011, Australia
FRANCE	Pergamon Press SARL, 24 rue des Ecoles, 75240 Paris, Cedex 06, France
WEST GERMANY	Pergamon Press GmbH, 3300 Braunschweig, Postfach 2923, Burgplatz 1, West Germany

First edition 1975

Library of Congress Cataloging in Publication Data

Philip, Alistair E
  Social work research and the analysis of social data

(The Commonwealth and international library)
Includes index.
1.   Social work education.   2.   Social service—
Research.   I.   McCulloch, James Wallace, 1921–
joint author.   II.   Smith, Norman James, joint author
III.   Title.
HV11.P592   1975   361   74–32369
ISBN 0–08–018213–5
ISBN 0–08–018212–7 pbk.

Printed in Great Britain by A. Wheaton & Co., Exeter

TO LORNA, ANNE AND ROBIN

Contents

Editor's Foreword

THIS book is written mainly for social workers but those in teaching, counselling, and other helping professions will find it useful. It is a book on research which describes both methodology and data analysis in logical sequence which is necessary as a basis in order to embark on the application of scientific method to psycho-social problems. Research begins when we try to fit observed phenomena into a logical framework. Sometimes an element seems not to fit into such a scheme and it is an exception such as this that often receives most attention in the hope that examination of it will lead to its inclusion within the framework. For instance, to take an example which links the helping professions, it was the exceptions who did not respond to compulsory school attendance and who failed to conform to society's expectations which led to studies of unauthorised absence from school. The study of truancy revealed consistent patterns in those who were absenting themselves from the educational process but more detailed study again showed an exceptional minority who did not absent themselves from home while absenting themselves from school. Other research workers were then able to study elements within this group and it became possible to define a specific sort of absence which became known as school phobia. Samples of different "populations" could then be taken for examination and planned statistical studies could be made. Hypotheses could be formulated and validated, and definitive statements made. Conjunctions of factors could be observed which, when acting coincidentally, would bring about the condition. A scientific principle then could follow. This is of importance in itself and also gives impetus for other studies either in greater breadth or in more detail. Each stage in the research process builds on what has gone before and there need be no artificial split between problem formation, methodology and analysis of the data.

For most professional people, whether in medicine, psychology, nursing, teaching, or social work, it is a major step to begin to undertake research. Yet each professional group needs soundly constructed studies which help in expanding their knowledge which can then be put to use in the service of others. This book by no means underestimates the difficulty of this step but with it the step becomes possible to take.

JEAN P. NURSTEN

Acknowledgements

We would like to thank our typists, Mrs. E. Donaldson and Miss S. Hartley, for preparing the typescript of this book. We are grateful to Dr. P. G. Fawcett and to the Editor and publishers of the *British Journal of Preventive and Social Medicine* for permission to incorporate the paper entitled "Some factors affecting the prevalence of stammering" in Chapter 13.

Introduction

THE field of social work is well endowed with theories which aim to account for why people behave as they do. Some theories, and indeed some parts of some theories, have greater practical utility than others. Unfortunately, each social worker has to find this out for herself, since theories are taught *in vacuo* without being put to the empirical test. The attitudes which social workers display towards statistics, or any move to count and measure what they do, may be seen as a consequence of, or a causal factor in, this position. Such attitudes are generally negative and can be viewed from different theoretical positions. From the Piagetian viewpoint this lack of numeracy would suggest that social workers utilise very basic concepts of number: one, two, a few, a lot. Freudian theory would suggest that such negative attitudes are irrational, emotionally charged and neurotic. In general learning theory terms such attitudes could be seen as learned responses which have been acquired.

Although this negative attitude to numeracy has led social work to a position where theories appear to be more highly valued than empirically ascertained facts, it is only recently that it has been seen for what it is, a crippling handicap. Recent legislation has made it possible for social work to flourish as never before, but to do so it must compete with other personal and public services for its share of local authority funds. Some of the legislation has, indeed, made research mandatory, and social work directors have to produce facts and figures about their departments, where the demands for their services come from and how efficaciously they are dealt with. Where the spending of public money is concerned, facts speak more eloquently than theories.

What we are suggesting here is that social workers, in order to advance their professional and theoretical aims, must work through any irrational attitudes towards counting and measuring. The proper use of descriptive and evaluative statistics can provide a body of empirical knowledge which complements and interacts with theory—both are necessary in any discipline.

The statistical approach to human and social problems has a number of advantages which can profitably be utilised by those wishing to acquire a greater understanding of personal problems. Accurate description is essential to any discipline; mathematics and statistics, with their special kinds of words, more precise than others we use, permit exact description. Because the language of statistics is exact, those who use the language become more precise and definite when they consider any phenomena, even in non-statistical terms. If, for instance, an agency worker is attempting to compare the kinds of problems which come to her rather than to another agency, then before she can carry out the comparison, a statistical procedure, she must decide what kind of contact constitutes a case, which problems can be grouped together and which must be kept apart, and many similar decisions. The decision to use even simple "head-counting" in a number of categories leads to the need for precision in thinking about people.

Statistics allow us to bring order to observations, to provide meaningful and convenient summaries of what has been done in an area. More important, we can use statistical techniques to go beyond mere description and summary; we can make inferences about findings and make predictions about future events based on such inferences.

Many public bodies, including social work agencies, produce masses of figures as part of annual reports and the like. Although such figures are often used to influence policy decisions, with even a modicum of more detailed analysis many more useful conclusions and predictions could be made. Knowledge of statistics should not be regarded as the province of a small body of research workers, it is something that everyone working in a profession which has its basis in social and behavioural science should know about. Even though a minority of social workers may conduct research, all social workers should be able to evaluate published research.

In this book we will present all the basic procedures which a social worker would require to conduct or evaluate empirical enquiries, to test the veracity of theoretical propositions or to evaluate the efficacy of some aspects of her own work or other people's reported studies.

Because statistics are only a part of the research process, some of our attention will be devoted to considering the role of research in current social work practice, the basics of research method and the transformation of clinical problems into research studies. The statistical procedures presented vary in their complexity and will include descriptive measures such as averages and scatter of scores, differences between measures, simple associations between variables, and two methods of analysis, typal analysis and dimensional analysis. We would emphasise that since the book is intended basically as a "primer" in research methods it is possible to conduct useful studies without the need to use the more complicated techniques of analysis given towards the end of the statistical section. However, these latter techniques do give the social scientist a wider appreciation of his own material and a greater ability to assess the work of others than would be attained by only using the more simple methods presented.

The rationale for the production of this book at this particular point in time is that there has been a very rapid growth in the social work profession in recent years and a growing recognition of the need for research to enhance practice. If the results of the efforts of researchers are to have the most positive effect on the social work profession they must be "consumed" objectively and critically. It is for these reasons that we have written for both the producer and the consumer.

CHAPTER 1

Professionalism and Empirical Research

IN this chapter we will endeavour to examine the interrelationship of *true* professionalism and the need to conduct research in the field of social work. It would appear to be logical in dealing with this topic to begin by discussing *professionalism*, to follow this with a discussion of *research* and then to synthesise these two. In addition, we will discuss the progress of research in this field, the opposition to this progress and finally the present situation.

What is a Profession?

There does not appear to be any generally accepted body which decides what occupations shall be classed as *professions*. The term profession is used by many people in different contexts and is often dependent on social class, status and occupation. Whilst it seems to be generally accepted that medicine, law and the church are professions, the agreement on other occupations is harder to reach when discussing the relative merits of, for example, auctioneers, radio engineers or social workers.

Historically it would appear that the development of the accepted professions mentioned earlier started with bodies of people acting from a vocation who pursued their work from a *desire* to do what they did rather than from any attached pecuniary gain. Over a period of time this was subject to change as younger "vocational" workers entered the sphere of work but coupled with some formal training and practical expertise gained from a body of knowledge which had built up through the years in an *ad hoc* manner.

1

The changes were brought about as the need for an accepted profession was realised by society at large and placed on a more remunerative footing, thus raising it and placing it in competition with other of the better paid occupations. In turn, this change meant that, in addition to higher remuneration, the "accepted" professions attracted more people whose interests derived not only from a *desire* to practice but also because of the favourable "living" offered.

As a result of this influx of interested people a mechanism of selection became the means necessary to control the numbers of aspirants. This selection procedure involved the creation of *standards* of entry which were based on the profession's *notional* level of the basic knowledge required to fulfill the *notional* professional task.

Once accepted as a noviate within the professional body, sets of rules and codes of conduct together with formal training in the practice of the profession ensured that the *notional* standards were enhanced and perpetuated.

Some writers on this topic itemise the characteristics of professional bodies thus:

1. Personal service to others (clients, patients, etc.) for a fixed remuneration fee or salary.
2. Prolonged specialised intellectual training coupled with supervised practice.
3. Machinery for setting and testing standards of competence and conduct.
4. Responsibility for the professional techniques involved and for the practice of colleagues in the profession.

Whilst it can be argued that the characteristics of "the professional" mentioned above could be applied to many occupations, differences of emphasis and focus are responsible for the fact that some occupations are called *professions* whilst others are not. Those occupations whose service to others involves life and death or privileged communication situations are said to be the most truly professional and these would include the examples given earlier, i.e. medicine, law and the church.

Many occupations nowadays require lengthy specialist training, but a major difference in the classification between occupation and profession is that the latter must qualify under all items in the list given.

But the main factor (item 2) which is common to both occupations and professions clearly does not establish by itself the right to be called a professional.

In both cases there has to be a body of knowledge peculiar to the occupation or professions, but there is a major difference between the two. The knowledge of the accepted professions is basically scientific—medicine, or institutional—law and theology. This knowledge is either created for or applied to the client or patient involved, but it is not part of the professional process that the acquired knowledge be for the prime purpose of communicating it to the patient or client so that he may use it independently. That is to say the accepted professional may communicate knowledge to his client, but this is within the context of the professional skill and situation within which the client or patient finds himself. This differs from other specially trained persons because it is concerned with people rather than things.

Social workers would appear to qualify under the terms listed to be professional people, but it cannot to date be said that they are truly professional. While the public at large accepts that the doctor has control over life and death situations, the degree to which they accept social workers, though considerable, is not so complete despite the fact that in many situations social workers do have such control. However, more important is the fact that though social workers in their training draw knowledge from other disciplines, they have no substantial knowledge base which is peculiarly their own. But this is not to deny the necessity for any profession to draw upon knowledge from other relevant sources and disciplines. In addition, despite the fact that social workers may strive for and achieve high standards for a professional nature, this is presently not necessary in order to practice as a social worker.

Whilst there is a machinery to impose tests of competence regarding specific social work qualifications, ranging from certificates to university degrees, there are no obligatory tests required for entry to the field of social work. It has been said that social work, together with teaching and nursing, are "semi-professions", since they often have skills more compatible with administrative occupations and that the qualities of their tasks are more focused on the direct communication of knowledge rather than creating or applying this specifically in the client/worker relationship. We would strongly dispute this on the grounds that while the aim of the social worker may be to help the client to change, the techniques involved in this enabling process are not communicated directly to the client and to this extent she is like the accepted professional. It seems by our argument that the major differences between social work as a "profession" and other professions lies in the paucity of specific social work knowledge.

This unique knowledge is necessary for many reasons: it enhances the service given to clients, it raises personal knowledge and therefore practice standards, it produces a corporate body of specific professional knowledge against which training standards can be measured, professional techniques enhanced, and leads to the creation of responsibility for all professional practice. Despite the need for such specific knowledge in social work, this is an area which is constantly neglected by the "profession". It is also the area to which research can contribute most.

What is Research?

By nature man is an enquiring and inquisitive animal with a desire to know or understand for its own sake or to apply the knowledge in order to do something better or more efficiently. In general, research is a process which seeks to acquire knowledge of a particular situation in an ordered manner.

The major goal of research is to provide information conducive to the creation of "laws" which will facilitate the explanation of perceived difficulties and thus enable predictions to be made. In order to achieve this, one has to be concerned to ensure that the information or facts which are gathered are reliable, and it should be realised that that which determines a fact can be a very complex matter. Not everyone is prepared to accept scientifically gathered facts and there must be some basis for people to make rational decisions about what they will accept in their questioning of the validity of factual evidence offered.

According to Labovitz and Hagedorn (1971) there are three common bases for establishing the validity of facts by persons not versed in scientific method:

1. Authority (a teacher, parent or expert says it is so).
2. Intuition (you just know it is so and you accept it).
3. Logic (it follows according to specified rules).

These authors emphasise that because each of these criteria can lead to false conclusions, it is necessary to use a more rigorous approach— the scientific method which is based on reliable and careful observation.

Labovitz and Hagedorn rightly point to the necessity of establishing causality before scientific laws can be established and they have suggested that the most widely accepted criteria for establishing this are *association, time priority, non-spurious relation* and *rationale*.

But in the field of social work research the establishment of causal relationships from a series of necessarily complex facts is by no means easy. Because of this, one has to avoid the pitfall of inferring cause and effect before the complexity of the facts involved have been unravelled.

Indeed, since social workers are really only in the very early stages of their creation of knowledge it may be necessary to unravel what are facts before seeking for causal relationships between facts. This is particularly so since, up to the present, there has been a tendency to accept theoretical concepts as though they were established uncomplicated facts.

Put into a social work context, research is concerned with the procedure which takes the clinical problem—the one met in practice— formalises and makes more explicit the area for investigation and then proceeds to study it in an objective, replicable manner.

The problem (or experienced difficulty) must be carefully formulated. That is, it must be translated in such a way as to enable it to be rigorously examined. Thinking about it, reading about it and talking about it with other people in a general way helps to establish whether or not it is a worthwhile idea and helps to crystallise and sharpen the topic. More formal reading is then needed to ascertain the current state of knowledge in the field. This is done by systematically searching the literature and recording the substance of the papers and books read in a form which will allow easy access to its contents and will carry a full reference for use in publication. Chapter 4 shows how this is done.

Papers and books vary in their worth and must therefore be read critically in order to assess their value in relation to the particular problem under investigation. Having formulated ideas for research, it is advisable to have someone well versed in research to examine them critically. This second opinion can save much wasted labour by pointing out errors of omission or commission before the study has got under way.

The basis of this process is the scientific approach to the study of phenomena. It has been argued by some social workers that one cannot be objective about people, but psychologists have long since recognised that when the organism being studied insists on being a person the realm of "pure" science must be left behind. But unlike many social workers they have not tended to reason from this that because we have left pure science behind we have also left behind the possibility of valid knowledge being gained by the scientific method.

When one recalls our definition of research and relates it to the brief outline of the process given, it can be seen that this process is little different to that involved in the good practice of social work in any sphere. In short, research means to search again for truth and fact in an orderly manner so that substantive communicable knowledge is acquired. Relating this, for example, to the casework process one can observe a similar pattern—an attempt is made to understand the client's problem in as clear a manner as is possible and then to translate this into diagnostic statements which can be communicated to others. It is then possible to test these statements by planned treatment involving deliberate techniques whose outcomes can be observed by the manner in which the client reacts to them. Equally with difficult cases one shows responsibility by discussing the case with experts or others who might throw some light on the situation or reference is made to relevant literature. The reason for process recording is to enable the worker to "research" or "look again" at what has been going on so that the client can be better understood. This casework process, if properly organised, can not only enhance the service to the client but its value can be communicated to other social workers. This is research.

In our discussion about professionalism we maintained that the basis of a professional status depended, amongst other things, on the existence of a body of knowledge peculiar to the profession. We have also indicated that to date there is a dearth of such knowledge and that this knowledge *is* necessary before social workers can truly be said to be professionals.

It has been argued that social workers are neither motivated nor have the necessary skills to conduct research, but it has been shown by Thomas, McCulloch and Brown (1969) that neither of these arguments holds good. As we have indicated, the nature of good social work practice is based on the ability to enquire and research in an ordered manner into the client's needs and into the techniques which are available and appropriate to meet these needs and then to assess the efficiency and efficacy of decisions made in the treatment transactions. In short, we see the social worker with his skills of interviewing and practice as being ideally suited to both consume and conduct research. Too often in the past the organisation of projects in the field of human relations has been left to other disciplines, although frequently the work has been carried out by persons with social work training. The result of this has been that the findings from such joint studies have added to the knowledge base of other disciplines with only secondary consequences for social workers. We are not arguing that social workers should "go it alone". Indeed we would argue strongly for a multi-disciplinary team approach as often as possible, but we see no reason why social workers should not be in a position to design a project and to be able to supervise its conduct.

The Progress of Research in Social Work

Research in social work has up to this point in time been relatively neglected in comparison to the development of social theories. However, developments in the broad field of social policy, such as the recommendations of the Seebohm Report (Department of Health and Social Security, 1968) and the national requirement of local authorities to survey the elderly and infirm, have highlighted not only the lack of knowledge but also the lack of expertise. This is amplified even further by the government's requirement of local authorities to furnish a "ten-year plan" for their proposed services and there is little doubt that what the Secretary of State for Health and Social Services will receive will be "guesstimates" rather than estimates. This is because of a failure to monitor existing services in years gone by which would have provided base lines from which to project "expected" trends.

At this level we refer only to knowing who the clients are and how many. We have not begun to try to assess the success of treatments in relation to the taught treatments methods and techniques, let alone to understand the processes that are involved.

Although there is a general dearth of social work research, there has fairly recently been an upsurge of research product on various aspects of practice which include studies on casework practice, fostering and adoption, handicapped children, delinquency, child abuse and the organisational problems surrounding the social services. Nevertheless, such research as has been done has been mainly at the agency or community survey level, rather than studies designed to test social work theories. Stein (1958) put this succinctly when he reminded social workers that "research is not social work research unless it is oriented to the development of social work theory or practice".

Whilst agency research is important in terms of agency practice and service to the client or the community, much of it derives from experience and local knowledge rather than from basic theory. According to Sucgang (1967), "in social work the goal of most applied research is, in general, to improve service or to determine the effects of a specific program on specific clients". Herzog (1959) has indicated that in order to evaluate work a series of questions must be asked:

1. What is the purpose of the evaluation?
2. What kind of change is desired?
3. By what means is the change to be brought about?
4. How trustworthy are the categories or measures to be employed?
5. At what point is change to be measured?
6. How fairly do the individuals studied represent the change discussed?
7. What is the evidence that the changes observed are due to the means employed?
8. What is the meaning of the changes found?
9. Were there any unexpected consequences?

As we have indicated, this sort of process is common to research and social work practice. In the former case results are being quantified to add to the store of knowledge, while in the latter it is used to enhance the treatment process. But there is little doubt that though the research aspect must be more rigorous and more methodical, these processes are similar. The problem is that if it is not systematically recorded the experience gained from the field of practice can never be tested for elements of commonality or difference.

This failure may have stemmed from the common philosophical assumption which underlies the thinking of many social workers that all clients are totally "unique". We would argue that any individual man is like all men, like some men, like no other man. The unique element is acknowledged, but the other two aspects are important elements which have to be understood before one can identify that which is unique. This necessitates the comparison of clients and the matching and testing of techniques used in relation to problems presented.

Although social work departments have established research sections, their products have been almost exclusively of an operational nature. This activity, while useful for policy formulation, has contributed little to the enhancement of social work practice and professional knowledge. Because of these deficiencies the social work "profession" has left itself open to serious criticism.

Opposition to Social Work Research

Not unnaturally some of the opposition to the progress of social work research has come from social workers themselves and we are all familiar with the sometimes sarcastic form that this takes:

"Social workers deal with people not figures."

"Lies, damned lies and statistics", etc.

Sometimes the internal opposition is in terms of resistance to the acquisition of research skills, the inapplicability of research findings for current practice, the unsuitability of the social worker to indulge in research or the absence of training for research.

These feelings have "fed" those who refuse to accept social work as a *true profession* and have tended to reinforce the feeling of other accepted professionals that social workers must be subordinate to them. For example, the observations of the Porritt Committee (Social Assay, 1963) included the suggestion that social workers were unsatisfactory in that they had a tendency to develop their own ideas on training and function without sufficient control by the medical profession. Training programmes, they said, had become too long and too complex and that this tendency must be checked. Another example of the onslaught on social work—the profession—came from Lady Wooton (1959) who said that social work should concern itself with doing for the ordinary citizen what private secretaries do for the selected few.

Without addressing themselves to the elements earlier outlined as the prerequisite of professionalism, there can be few grounds on which social workers can contest the cynics. We can go a long way towards meeting such criticisms by learning how to accumulate and understand valid, systematically acquired knowledge in the social work field. How this can be done is the nexus of this book.

References

DEPARTMENT OF HEALTH AND SOCIAL SECURITY (1968) *Report of the Committee on Local Authority and Allied Personal Social Services.* London: H.M.S.O. (Seebohm Report).

HERZOG, E. (1959) *Some Guide Lines for Evaluative Research.* Washington, D.C.: Department of H.E.W.

LABOVITZ, S. and HAGEDORN, R. (1971) *Introduction to Social Research.* New York: McGraw-Hill.

SOCIAL ASSAY (1962) *Review of the Medical Services in Great Britain.* London: Social Assay. (Porritt Committee).

STEIN, H. D. (1958) Chapter in *Social Science in Social Work* (Ed. H. J. Parad). New York: Family Service Association of America.

SUCGANG, R. R. (1967) Research and the production of professional literature in social work education. *Graduate and Faculty Studies,* Vol. XVII. Mendiola, Manila: Centro Escolar University.

THOMAS, E. J., McCULLOCH, J. W. and BROWN, M. J. (1969) An experiment to evaluate research instruction for undergraduate social workers. *App. Soc. Studies,* **1,** 93–105.

WOOTON, B. (1959) *Social Science and Social Pathology.* London: Allen & Unwin.

CHAPTER 2

Why Count and Measure?

VARIOUS reactions by social workers to the findings of social work and allied research have been hypothesised. It is often assumed that the social worker will continue in professional practice unaffected by the implications of research findings and that these findings will either be ignored, rejected or modified to fit existing theories. Much of this rather negative judgement of social workers has rested largely on *a priori* reasoning and not upon empirical study. As we have already indicated, there has been some reluctance in the social work profession to participate in research and to systematise factors pertinent to the helping process.

This resistance to the intrusion of research into the social work situation can be both justified and appreciated, but may be explained by a general attitude towards change and the anxiety that change frequently generates. This is not to say that, over the years, the social work profession has been static. This would be far removed from the truth, but the changes which have occurred have tended to be non-empirically based modifications of existing theories which were themselves non-empirically based and thus likely to be less threatening.

Because of the recent alteration in the structure of the social services a greatly increased number of decisions of an operational nature have to be taken. These decisions may be with regard to the handling of clients, staff, allocation of cases, administration and the like. Few agencies would consciously want to make important decisions based only on faith, and so it has become imperative that we begin to learn how to make the fullest use of the accessible information in all these areas in order to ensure that decisions are knowledge based. It makes good sense to base decision-making on reality where this is possible and social work research is a very impartial and systematic way of getting at social work reality. Research has a logical, rational appeal which cannot be denied on any intellectual level, and we are certain that social workers can learn to know their profession at least as well as any other social scientists. Further, we believe that *only* social workers can possibly accept the responsibility for continuing agency-based research.

It is recognised that in social work research the requisites of "production" are not identical to those of "consumption". The producer must have acquired numerous skills in order to carry out research. These skills include conceptualisation, problem formulation, research design, the development of data-gathering techniques, statistical computation and decision-making and the interpretation of results. The consumer of research need not possess these particular skills, but he must understand selected basic principles and be able properly to appraise the results of studies.

In this book we make the assumption that all social workers should school themselves into becoming intelligent consumers of research since the behaviours which constitute "intelligent consumption", like most complex behaviours, must be acquired through learning. It is not suggested that all social workers become producers of research. Indeed, it may be that only a modest proportion of social workers will, or even should, become researchers, since mostly they enter into the field because they wish to become practitioners or administrators.

In this book it is the authors' intention to attempt to ensure that the reader will be able to learn how to consume research at a modest level and that social workers with special interest in participating in empirical research will receive sufficient instruction to be able to fulfil the skills mentioned earlier. It could be argued that research in social work is still a relatively unproven skill, but it is precisely for this reason that the state of the research skills available to us must be learned, for only in this way can there be progress towards the proof of its value.

Since this book is concerned with aiding the understanding of statistical procedures, and because we are sensible to the negative feelings that the word "statistics" tends to arouse among social workers and those in allied professions, it becomes immediately necessary to discuss the advantages of counting and measuring. This is particularly so because a major criticism which has been levelled at the social work researcher has been that because he is interested in figures he cannot really be interested in people. It is important to learn sooner rather than later that research, involving as it does some understanding of statistics, helps the social worker to become a better, rather than a worse, practitioner regardless of his area of practice.

The statistical approach to human and social problems certainly has at least six distinct advantages that can be utilised by social workers and by others who seek a greater understanding of the problems in which *people* are involved.

These are:

1. Statistics permit the most exact kind of description of phenomena.
2. The statistical approach forces us to be definite and exact in our procedures and in our thinking.
3. Statistics enable us to summarise our results in a meaningful, unambiguous and convenient form.
4. Statistics enable us to quantify observations and permit the drawing of general conclusions.
5. Statistics enable us to make predictions about future events and to test the accuracy of such predictions. It is only when we reach this stage that one can begin to think of preventive regimes and to instigate and monitor changes in practice.
6. Statistics enable us to analyse some of the causal factors of complex and otherwise bewildering events.

In the social sciences, statistics can serve as an important tool for a number of purposes all of which, for the social worker especially, need ultimately to be utilised to effect a more efficient service for the profession's clientele.

Statistics as such have no intelligence of their own. They have to be collected, collated, analysed and interpreted in order to make sense to the researcher so that the resultant knowledge may be sufficiently clear for that knowledge to be communicated to the "consumer" and to other researchers who would question the results or use them in such a way that would help them to formulate a more advanced problem or to repeat the project in some other area or with some other people.

It is often supposed that statistics will make sense on their own and that if sufficient data is fed into a computer something of great interest will emerge. Nothing could be further from the truth. Statistics only have value in so far as they are part of a plan to answer a particular problem or to supply information which is pertinent to a specific question. The manner in which data will be collected, analysed and interpreted will be determined largely by the nature of the problem being studied.

It is not possible, even with aid of the most modern computers, to collect all data about all things. Research is essentially a progression of small steps, and we need to be selective both as to the population, the specific group of subjects we intend to study, and the characteristics of that population. Even with these necessary limitations it is still remarkably easy to collect a bewildering mass of data, and so the essential task becomes one of ordering, counting and measuring them so that they become meaningful.

Masses of figures, in themselves, say almost nothing. Indeed, they can become extremely confusing since the human mind is incapable of consuming, let alone making meaningful interpretation of, vast quantities of disorderly data. Providing a study has been properly conducted, the resultant data have an important story to tell, but are rather like the separate pieces of a jig-saw puzzle in that they have to be properly put together to make a picture.

Like a jig-saw, the true picture can only emerge if the pieces are put into their proper places, and just as cutting pieces to make them fit will distort the picture, so it is with the improper handling of data. With a good jig-saw, attempts to interpret the whole picture from one piece amount to sheer guess-work and so it is with statistics. There is a danger that inaccurate generalisations might be drawn from specific situations or atypical samples if the rules of sound statistical analysis are not observed. It is equally dangerous, of course, to draw inferences from properly ordered and analysed data if the sample from the population from which these data evolved was a biased one, that is if the sample was atypical. For example, to assume knowledge about the population of one or all hospitals from the characteristics of the patients from one ward would be totally unjustified.

When data have been collected, it is usually necessary to count and measure them in ways which are accurate and meaningful, but in order to extract the fullest meaning the data have to be analysed using techniques which are appropriate to the task.

Counting tells us how many units we have of some particular population and measuring tells us how much there is of any particular quality. It is necessary, as was indicated in our introduction, to be sure that the units being counted are of a like kind and that the measuring instrument used does measure what it purports to measure. If we were concerned to find out the characteristics and caseload of the clients of a social work agency, we would certainly have to know how many clients there were. But before we could start counting we would have to accurately define the term "client". For example, it would be necessary to decide whether each member of a family with which the agency was working should be counted as one client; whether the person referred to the agency was the client or whether it was the family member with whom the social worker worked; whether a person who has had only one consultation is a client; or whether a person who has had no contact with the agency for some period of time is still a client and so on.

It is totally unsatisfactory to start to make definitions whilst in the process of counting in relation to problems as they are encountered; categories have to be created before the counting begins and there are four basic rules involved.

1. The categories used must be created in relation to the research problem and its purpose.

2. Categories must be exhaustive. There must be a category for every response from every respondent in the study. In doing this there can be safeguards against meeting an unforeseen response by, for example, creating a category called "other". One must also allow for categories such as "not applicable", "not known", "not answered", etc.

3. Each category must be mutually exclusive; no response should be capable of filling more than one category. It is for this reason that definition is of vital importance.

4. Each category must be derived from one classification principle and be on one level of discourse. If, for example, one wanted to categorise agency clients according to their area of residence, it would be necessary to devise a principle of classification such as electoral ward or polling district or some other clearly defined and constant unit.

It is essential to define all the elements before the count begins. It is unlikely that one would want to count clients physically and we would probably accept the case records as being accurate substitutes and count them instead—but even a simple decision of this order requires to be made at the outset.

If our interest is in the size of our clientele, we, after definition and counting, may arrive at a figure of, say, 1842. This overall figure, although of interest, is really too crude to be of any real value and some break-down into categories that will be of use to us becomes necessary. This break-down can only be obtained by going through all of the data again. It follows, therefore, that it is sound policy not only to define terms before making a beginning but also to determine the form of categorisation which will be of the greatest value to us. Why do we stress this elementary fact? Only as a result of much experience of wasted time in recounting data due to having given insufficient thought at the beginning as to the categories that were later required. With our 1842 clients, for example, we may be interested in a break-down by sex, age, marital status, social class, reason for referral, type of referral, type of problem, prognosis, etc. An example of a possible breakdown is given in Table 2.1.

With counting it is always much easier to group figures together than it is to separate them out. Better, therefore, to start off with too many categories than with not enough.

Categories can be combined in the counting stage, but if the combination is done before the data have been collected there is a serious risk of losing vital information. If, for example, we were interested in the social class of our clientele and we had decided to combine the categories into the Registrar General's classes 1 and 2, class 3 and classes 4 and 5 and had collected the data accordingly, we could arrive at the distribution shown in Table 2.2.

TABLE 2.1. AGENCY CLIENTELE BY SEX, AGE GROUPS AND TYPE OF
REFERRAL

	Self-referred Age group			Other-referred Age group			
Sex	0–5 years	5–15 years	over 15 years	0–5 years	5–15 years	over 15 years	Total
Male	0	76	109	322	493	116	1116
Female	0	52	80	491	32	71	726
Both sexes	0	128	189	813	525	187	1842

By combining the categories there is no way of becoming aware that none of the self-referred males in the social class category 1+2 belonged, in fact, to social class 1 while all of the females from the same group did. If the actual social class had been recorded, then this information would not have been lost.

A close look at the data presented in Tables 2.1 and 2.2 shows that the numbers of people in each group (self-referred and "other"-referred) are substantially different, and when these groups are further divided according to the sex and social class of the client, it becomes obvious that it is not easy to understand the data. It is difficult to decide if, for instance, the social class proportions of females in the two groups are different. There are 132 in the self-referred group and

TABLE 2.2. AGENCY CLIENTELE ACCORDING TO SEX, SOCIAL CLASS AND TYPE OF
REFERRAL

	Self-referred Social class			Other-referred Social class			
Sex	1 + 2	3	4 + 5	1 + 2	3	4 + 5	Total
Male	38	109	38	122	603	206	1116
Female	26	80	26	291	232	71	726
Both sexes	64	189	64	413	835	277	1842

594 in the "other"-referred group. Similarly, from the data presented
in Table 2.1, one has to calculate what the comparative proportions in
each compartment or *cell* are before any obvious comparisons can be
made.

When it is remembered that the results of research have to be consumed by persons who are often less skilled and less sophisticated in
research techniques than the researcher, then the findings or results
must be presented in the simplest and clearest manner. To achieve this
one can present the same data as percentages of the total numbers of
persons involved so that quick and easy comparisons may be made. If
we convert the data from Table 2.2 into percentages (Table 2.3) there is
more clarity.

TABLE 2.3. AGENCY CLIENTELE ACCORDING TO SEX, SOCIAL CLASS AND TYPE OF
REFERRAL (PERCENTAGES)

Sex	Self-referred Social class			Other referred Social class			Total
	1 + 2	3	4 + 5	1 + 2	3	4 + 5	
Male	3.41	9.77	3.41	10.93	54.03	18.46	100.00
Female	3.58	11.02	3.58	40.08	31.96	9.78	100.00
Both sexes	3.47	10.26	3.47	22.42	45.33	15.04	100.00

At a glance it can now be seen that for male clientele there is a far
greater difference in the social class 3 "other"-referred group than in
the self-referred group, and that to a lesser extent this finding holds
good for women. We can see too that while there is little difference
between the proportions of social class 1+2 women in the "other"-
referred group there is a vast difference in the proportions of the male
population in the same group.

An important warning here. A percentage of one group of figures
should never be added to a percentage from another. Example, 10% of
116 is not the same as 10% of 726, and our resultant "20%" total
would not be a 1/5 (20%) of either group.

As a rule percentages should not be used in dealing with totals of less than 100. With small totals, each unit carries a large amount of the percentage and this can give an erroneous impression. For example, a group of four people are talking together and one person leaves the group. We could say that the group had been reduced by 25%, but it probably gives a more accurate picture to say that the group had been reduced by one person. It is also important when percentages are used to indicate this in the title of the table.

As well as counting data we are likely to want to obtain some measurement of certain of their characteristics or *attributes*. We may be concerned to attempt to measure the progress a client has made within the casework relationship, the effectiveness of the seminar group as a teaching method or the extent of racial prejudice within a neighbourhood. In the physical world we measure much phenomena with readily-available measuring instruments. We measure with a rule, with a weighing machine, with a thermometer, with a voltage meter and so on. In the social sciences, few such reliable measuring tools have been developed. In many instances we are obliged to develop our own instruments in order to conduct a particular piece of research. There are certain general rules and guidelines that can be used in their construction. The definition of measurement can be taken as *the assignment of numbers of objects and events according to logically accepted rules*, and within the terms of this definition, the construction of specific instruments can be quite legitimate.

The types of instruments that we can construct will be limited by the type of data with which we are dealing. The simplest but most limiting type of data, so far as measurement is concerned, is *nominal data*. This in essence is "Yes–No" data. If, for example, we are interested in racial origin, we may categorise data on a European–Non-European scale. If a person is not "Yes" to the first category, then he automatically belongs to the second category. This *is* a scale, albeit a simple one, as a scale is defined as "that which discriminates". We might choose to give numbers to our categories such as group 1 and group 2, but this numbering would be quite arbitrary. The nominal scale deals with qualitative data and this data is not on any form of continuum.

Much of the data measured by social scientists is known as *ordinal data* and is measured on an ordinal scale. This is *quantitative* type data measured on a continum. *Ordinal data* possess a *"more than–less than"* characteristic and thus can be rank ordered. Joe responds to casework treatment better than Bill but not as well as Tom. Mike responds less well than Bill. Thus, our rank order of positive response to casework treatment would be:

Client	Rank
Tom	1
Joe	2
Bill	3
Mike	4

There would be nothing to indicate, however, that the "distance" between Tom and Joe was the same as the "distance" between Joe and Mike. Ordinal data gives us a rank ordering only, it tells us nothing about the distance between units and permits wide discrepancy of distances between units.

Although much of the material handled by workers in the field of human science naturally falls into the ordinal scale category, we attempt where possible to develop scales which have distances of equal intervals and relate the observed data to a point on this scale. If we measure one piece of wood with a tape measure and it measures 15 inches and we measure a second piece of wood and it measures 30 inches, then we can say, quite correctly, that the second piece of wood is twice as long as the first. The reason for this statement is that the second 15 inches of our measuring instrument covers exactly the same distance as the first 15 inches. When a teacher is marking essays and she gives a mark of 40%, this should mean that it is 4/10ths along the way of a continuum which the teacher is using to measure the student's work. It should also mean that the essay is exactly twice as good as the essay that was awarded a mark of 20%, but only half as good as the essay that was awarded a mark of 80%. In reality this is often not the case, but the teacher wants to give the appearance of *interval scale* precision. In fact, he is only handling the data in an *ordinal* way. The highest type of measurement, from a statistical standpoint, is known as ratio data, which can properly be measured on a ratio scale. A *ratio scale* not only has the quality of an interval scale but also has a meaningful absolute zero point.

According to Siegel (1956) a ratio scale has been thus defined: "When a scale has all the characteristics of an interval scale and in addition has a true zero point as the origin, it is called a ratio scale. In a ratio scale, the ratio of any two scale points is independent of the unit of measurement."

In the social sciences very little data can be legitimately measured on a ratio scale, but one example of such a scale can be seen in Table 2.1 where one variable or dimension of the table deals with age. When dealing with age (in years) there is an absolute zero point and, in addition, an age scale has all the characteristics of an interval one.

Reference

SIEGEL, S. (1956) *Nonparametric Statistics for the Behavioural Sciences.* New York: McGraw-Hill.

CHAPTER 3

The Research Process

IN Chapter 1 a brief outline of what is involved in a research programme was outlined. This chapter will deal more specifically with the various steps involved and will do so in greater depth. We must emphasise, however, that although this presentation is given under specific headings, each step is to some extent dependent on the others. It is our intention to give the reader sufficient information to understand what is involved in the research process but at a fairly elementary level. There are many books which deal with the subject matter of this chapter at much greater depth, and references to some of these works are listed at the end of the chapter.

The Formulation of a Problem

The types of problems or perceived difficulties met in the field of social work cover a very wide range, from the descriptive account to the testing of the validity of statements about the relationship between two or more factors. The latter is known as *hypothesis testing*.

One of the bases for undertaking work in the social work field is the value that the social worker places on certain factors in life. It can be from these values or beliefs that discrepancies between what *is* and what *ought to be* lead to questions being asked about which there appears to be no obvious or immediate answer. One important source of such questioning has, for social workers, frequently arisen from their observations of client/social worker interactions. Such *case studies* are extremely valuable as insight-stimulating and hypothesis-generating sources. Not infrequently, depth studies of single cases can provide the origins of valuable theoretical concepts which, until empirical testing is possible, can be perfectly valid bases for subsequent professional practice. A classical example of this approach is demonstrated by the works of Sigmund Freud. In the social work field the case study approach has been extensively used and some examples of this method are shown as "Recommended Reading" at the end of this chapter. However, it could simply be that questions arise which are little more than "hunches", or ideas which spring from written words, conversations, theoretical statements and so on. Indeed, the seeds of questioning may arise from almost anywhere.

For example, over the years there have been critics of the social work profession who have questioned the need for the training that social workers receive or, indeed, the need for any training at all. One way to try to provide an answer to such criticism or to show that the criticism was a valid one would be to conduct research in order to find out the truth of the matter, and to do this the problem to be investigated would have to be stated in a manner amenable to research. Such a study could take the form of the measurement of the effectiveness of social work contacts with clients comparing a group of workers who have been professionally trained with a group of workers who had had no training.

There is no priority for the sources of problems, although perhaps there ought to be priority for the conduct of research in terms of which studies ought to be undertaken first, this priority being based on the utility they have in relation to social work in terms of the timing of the study and the particular stage of development of the profession.

Having decided an area for investigation, the next step in the process is to discuss the idea with colleagues and other interested people, especially with persons who are liable to be well versed in the particular area or in the field of research generally. Such discussion leads to a sharpening of focus and highlights possible difficulties that might be met and can lead to the production of pertinent ideas which might otherwise be overlooked in the development of a specific topic within the area of investigation.

It is very important in thinking about a possible area and a specific topic to find out what previous related and relevant work on the subject has been done. Such works may stem from learned discussion, empirical studies, general unformulated ideas and theoretical concepts. The search of the literature should not be confined to the social work field, but must include related spheres of influence such as medicine, psychiatry, criminology, sociology and psychology.

From the literature one is not only learning about the present state of knowledge but also about methods and techniques which have been previously used either successfully or unsuccessfully. If successful they can be replicated, and if not they can be modified or avoided. Reading also helps to clarify the topic and allows the researcher to begin to think about it in workable dimensions. It also offers the would-be researcher a variety of ways of observing and conceptualising the proposed area for study. Literature searching itself involves the use of rigorous methodology and a much more detailed description of how this should be approached is given in Chapter 4.

Having thoroughly searched the literature and discussed the topic with others, one is now ready to state, in global terms, the *aims* of the study. This is a brief statement of the topic to be studied, why it has been chosen for study and what its usefulness and relevance will be to the body of social work knowledge. Again using our example of the effectiveness of social work practice in relation to training, the *aims* of such a study might be expressed in the following manner:

EXAMPLE 1

The aim of this study is to examine the effectiveness of social work transactions undertaken by social workers to see if training has any effect on the outcome of the transaction in terms of client functioning over a specified period of time and in relation to the amount of contact during that time. By conducting this research it is hoped to provide factual information which will enable more considered decisions to be made regarding the employment and deployment of social workers and to assist in the development of future training policies in relation to social work practice needs.

Underlying the study is an assumption that present professional training based on specific relationship theories is more effective in social work than no training or training of some other kind.

Having delineated the boundaries of the study, the specifics or *objects* may now be stated. These constitute the *hypotheses* which it is proposed to test in order to confirm or refute, in this case, the critics' contention.

It is conventional, though not obligatory, to state hypotheses which are the opposite of the researcher's own beliefs about the statement. This is known as the *"Null"* form of hypothesising. The underlying rationale for so doing is based on the logic that a law is only a law for so long as it cannot be disproved. In the example given we would adopt the critics' contention and then proceed to try to disprove it. If the study results then did not disprove conclusively what the critics had postulated, we would be forced to accept that their statement was true in so far as the example study had been designed to test its veracity.

By stating hypotheses in a "null" manner the researchers' efforts will be more rigorous than might otherwise be the case, and he will be less likely to design, consciously or unconsciously, a study which would serve to support his beliefs. In other words the researcher's bias will be minimised to some degree.

Again using our example of social work effectiveness (Example 1) we would set out a hypothesis thus:

> *There will be no difference in the effectiveness of treatment between a group of professionally trained social workers and a group of untrained social workers.*

At the problem formulation stage it is necessary to ensure that each hypothesis or sub-hypothesis contains only a single element to be tested and to guard against the possibility that even though the findings do show that there is some association between the variables under study that it is not a *spurious* one. That is, that an apparent relationship between two variables arises not from a connection between them but from the fact that each of them is related to another variable which does not cause the relationship in the form of a link. Where there is a link variable this would be known as an *intervening variable*. This occurs when a variable *A* is associated with a variable *B* because of the intervention of a third variable *C*. Using our social work effectiveness hypothesis, a research study could show that there was an association between professional training and effectiveness of social work, but it would be spurious if, in fact, the variables of age, sex and experience were involved but were not acting as links and had not been tested. It is rarely the case that in groups under study each person in any group will be like all other people in that group and in our study it might emerge that some members of the professionally trained group worked just as effectively as some of the members of the untrained group and that those who were alike had in common the factors of age, sex and experience (or any one of them). If this were so, then the apparent association between training and effectiveness could be spurious. For example, it could be that there was similarity in the level of effectiveness between professionally trained workers with x amount of experience and untrained workers with the same amount of experience and we would then have to question the seeming association between training and effectiveness and look more closely at the relationship between effectiveness and experience with or without training.

This is handled by attempting to foresee other factors or variables which might also colour effectiveness in social work practice and attaching them separately and severally under the main hypothesis as sub-hypotheses. Our effectiveness example would now be set out in the following manner:

> *There will be no difference in the effectiveness of treatment between a group of professionally trained social workers and a group of un-trained social workers.*

The above hypothesis will not be affected by any of the following *sub-hypotheses*:

(a) The age of the social worker.
(b) The sex of the social worker.
(c) The length of the social worker's experience in social work.

In this way we still have single elements which can separately be tested by the study design and conduct and, to some extent, the possibility of spurious associations has been diminished since in our analysis we could process the data in such a way as to show the presence of variables which did not act as links between variables which appeared to be associated.

When thinking through a problem, an important factor to be considered is the researcher's own self-discipline. This can be maintained by his continually addressing himself to the following questions:

1. Has the problem been specified in researchable terms?
2. Do the proposed hypotheses meet the standards of previous works resulting from a critical search of the literature?
3. Are the hypotheses formulated in a clear and concise manner and are they and any sub-hypotheses restricted to one element?
4. Where a theory underlies the work is this logically consistent?
5. Have the concepts and terms which are to be used in the study been clearly defined? Definitions may be concepts which express an abstraction formed by generalising from particular events. For example, in social casework the nature of the relationship between worker and client is based on a particular theory of interaction. In any particular study an operational definition may be selected from the literature or it may be deliberately invented. It could be that the term "relationship" is defined as "a condition where two persons with some common interest . . . interact with feeling".
    Whether the consumers of research or other researchers would necessarily agree with this definition is not at issue. What does matter is that it is known how the word "relationship" was being used and if it was desired to replicate the study, this could be done.

It will have become apparent to the reader by this stage that there are many operational decisions to be made and it is necessary not only to know what has been decided but when and why. In order to ensure that the process of any research project is not lost it is advisable to begin by recording all decisions, together with the reasons for them, in chronological order in a log book. By doing this one can then communicate to others the difficulties or advantages of the study design and methods used. This is also the point at which the researcher is ready to think about how he will approach the collection of the data that will test his hypotheses. This is the *design* stage.

Research Design

Involved in this stage are a number of processes which although considered separately are inter-related and continually re-assessed and modified as necessary. In the conduct of many projects it is possible and even advisable to carry out several of the stages at the same time. For example, consider a null hypothesis which stated.

EXAMPLE 2

There will be no difference in the number of cases which present at a social work agency according to the day of the week.

Clearly there would be no point in pursuing the design unless the agency concerned gave permission for its records to be used in order to obtain the data. At the same time it would be futile to approach the agency's director unless the reasons for the research and how it was proposed to conduct it could be discussed with him. The inter-relation of the steps involved which could possibly lead to a later stage modifying an earlier one will be clearer if yet another example of a null hypothesis is used.

EXAMPLE 3

There will be no difference between professionally trained social workers and untrained social workers in their attitudes towards the problems presented by clients.

In order to decide on the number of workers to include in this particular study consideration would have to have been paid to the analytic procedures which it had been proposed to use. This, in itself, requires a clarification of the definitions to be employed. That is, using Example 3, we should have to be clear which social workers in the sample were to be called "professional" and which to be called "untrained" and that there was a sufficient number of each to satisfy the conditions necessary to justify the analytical techniques proposed. Using the same example it might be decided to use statistical tests which could only be used if the proposed sample were large enough.

Absence of a sufficient number of people to meet test requirements would necessitate a change of design in one or more ways.

(i) Another more appropriate test could be envisaged.

(ii) Definitions could be altered.

(iii) Sample size could be increased.

(iv) Categories could be combined.

Consideration of other aspects of the design steps might necessarily limit the alternatives or, more seriously, cause the project to be abandoned.

It is hoped that the foregoing discussion will have shown the importance of the elements of design and their relationship to each other. It is now our intention to discuss each element separately.

General Planning

According to Weiss (1968), "Study design refers especially to the kind of sample selected by the investigator and the degree of control over phenomena that the investigator possesses." He suggests that there are four main kinds of study design:

(a) The case study.

(b) Comparative research—this involves comparing the attitudes of one group of people with another.

(c) Survey research—the compilation of information concerning some area of interest. A good example of this would be opinion polls.

(d) Experiments—for instance if the following null hypothesis had previously been tested,

EXAMPLE 4

There will be no differences in the rates of identifiable indices of social malaise according to the geographical area of study,

and it was found that two geographical areas had the same rates of a particular index, one could then establish in one of them a new experimental unit. It would be possible after a period of time to observe the effectiveness of that unit on the specific index under study by comparing its rates with the rates for the same index in the area which had no unit.

Sampling

There are two main considerations which come under this heading:
(a) The type of the sample, and
(b) the size of the sample necessary for analysis.

SAMPLE TYPE

In a general sense there are two main types of sample. The first is known as a *probability sample*, in which it is possible to specify that for each element of the population to be studied there will be an equal chance for it to be included in the sample and therefore the size of the sample can be specified.

In probability sampling there are four main ways of selecting the sample for study:

(i) *Simple random sampling.* This is not random in the sense that units can be drawn from a hat or chosen with a pin. In the latter case the selected units would tend to be biased according to the handedness of the selector. What is meant in research terms by random is that every unit or combination of units has an equal chance of being selected. For example, if we have units *A, B, C, D* and *E*, each one would have an equal chance of being chosen as would the following combinations—*AB, AC, AD, AE* and so on.

(ii) *Stratified random sampling.* Using this method one would divide the total population into at least two clearly defined sections by single or multiple criteria such as age, sex or social class. This technique is used to ensure that the researcher gets a sample of each group which is sufficiently large enough to analyse. For example, if it was desired to look at a variable in relation to the social class of respondents we should have to select a very large number of people by the simple random method in order to get a sufficient number who belonged to social class I. This is because there are only two or three people in every hundred who could be so categorised. To reduce the sample number and to ensure sufficient numbers in each class category, we could draw a simple random sample from a list of each class separately until the numbers in each class were sufficiently large to analyse. That is until we saw fifty of each class or a total sample of two hundred and fifty as against the two thousand we should have to draw by the simple random procedure to be sure of getting fifty people in social class I.

(iii) *Cluster sampling*. This technique is normally used when money and time are in short supply. For example, if it was desired to conduct a study of a country's urban people for some reason, it would be very time consuming and costly to take a simple random sample from the whole country.

Instead, we could list and number every city in the country and by simple random selection choose one city to represent all cities. But this in itself could present the researcher with unmanageable numbers and so, repeating the procedure used to select the city for study a multi-stage operation could take the researcher from a randomly selected city to a randomly selected electoral or postal district within the city and from thence to a random selection of persons or households.

It will be obvious to the reader that, though it may be cheaper and less time consuming to work this way, it is less efficient than simple random sampling since it would be no longer true to say that every urbanised person in the country had an equal chance of being selected to participate in the study.

(iv) *Systematic sampling*. This technique is often confused with sample random sampling. It involves deciding the necessary sample size and selecting the sample by taking every *n*th case from the total population to be studied. Clearly, however, if it was decided to select every fifth person, the second, third and fourth person would have no chance of being selected.

Systematic sampling can either be a probability sample or a non-probability one. If, for example, we were interested in a group of people who had attempted suicide we could apply it to a hospital ward where all patients had behaved this way and we would, therefore, be sure that our systematic sample contained only attempted suicides or it could fall into the second main type of sampling which is known as *non-probability sampling*.

The basic difference between probability sampling and non-probability sampling is that for the latter we cannot develop a scale of confidence. To use the same example, we could determine from a total population of attempted suicides that the sample we drew represented the whole population with regard to, for example, age and calculate just how accurate this would be. But if we drew every *n*th case from all hospital admissions, we could not infer with any certainty that the mean age of the attempted suicides who appeared in the sample would be the mean age of a total population of attempted sucides, unless we were sure that the hospital case records were well enough mixed so as to permit the researcher to be less careful in his sampling procedure.

In addition to systematic sampling non-probability sampling has three other main types:

(i) *Accidental sampling.* In this sense accidental means simply to use the cases that are to hand.

(ii) *Quota sampling.* In this method we choose characteristics in the population which are believed to be associated with the variable under study and we deliberately try to make the sample a representative one in these aspects. If we believe that social class is a characteristic which is associated with attempted suicide, then we would construct a sample which was representative in this aspect.

(iii) *Purposive sampling.* The basic underlying principle in this type of sampling is that based on experience or good judgement one can select the cases to be included in the sample that will satisfy the needs of the study. For example, if it was desired to study the differences between a group of clients who presented an agency with seemingly intractable problems and a group whose problems seemed to respond to social work help, then one would simply select people who appeared to satisfy these conditions.

There are certain problems inherent in obtaining a truly representative sample and usually some compromises have to be made. It would not be feasible, for example, to obtain a complete random sample of social workers in the United Kingdom if there was not in existence a complete list of their names and addresses. A random selection of workers' names taken from the list of members of the British Association of

Social Workers might have to be accepted as being sufficiently representative of the whole profession.

As we have indicated, samples often have to be drawn by having recourse to random numbers. It is not possible to think truly in a random manner and so we cannot feel confident in just thinking about a number or by selecting numbers by the use of a pin. In the former we would not be likely to pick 9969 as a number since we would likely be tempted to knock out one of the nines while in the latter the numbers "pinned" might, as we indicated earlier, be dependent on the handedness of the "sticker".

Most statistics books have, as appendices, a table of numbers which have been selected randomly by a computer process and these are invaluable for the maintenance of the true random selection of units.

In working with a sample of a total population we are, in essence, stating that the sample values are compatible with the values of the population from which it was drawn at specific levels of probability. This involves the concepts of a *confidence interval* and a *confidence level*. The confidence interval is the range within which we assert that the true population value lies while the confidence level represents the chances of being wrong in that assertion.

We cannot say, for example, that the mean of a sample of clients' ages *ought*, if accurately drawn, to be 40 and be certain of being right; or even because a sample mean *is* 40, that the mean of the population of scores from which the sample was drawn will *be* 40 and be even 95 % certain of being right. We can only say that because the sample is 40, the population mean will fall between 40 $\pm$ 1, and be 95 % sure of being right. In other words, we can calculate a range—*the confidence interval* —within which the population mean is likely to fall and we can indicate the degree of confidence—*the confidence level*—which can be ascribed to the sample. We can have no idea, however, whether the true mean is nearer to 40 or to 41 and, by the laws of chance, in five times out of every hundred the mean could fall outside this range.

Data Analysis

In research design the sample size to be selected is extremely important for other reasons. We could select a sample which was large enough to have a minimum range of the confidence interval, but in design we are also concerned to decide in advance which techniques will be used to analyse the data gathered from the sample. It follows, therefore, that not only must the sample be large enough to represent the parent population with some certainty—usually 95% or greater— but it should also be large enough to satisfy the selected statistical methods which have been selected for analysis. If we wanted to know not just the average size of caseload of our sample of forty social workers but also if there was any association between caseload size and the age of social workers, we would have to create mutually exclusive categories of caseload size according to age. By doing this we could then apply a test of association such as the Chi-square test (see page 111) to find out if any observed association between the variables of age and caseload was one which could be purely a chance one or not. The use of the Chi-square test is governed by the numbers in each cell which would be expected if chance alone were operating, and if the numbers in the sample were insufficient for the test to be used then the test would have to be abandoned or the number of cells or categories reduced or the sample size would have to be increased. (This concept will be covered more readily in Chapter 8.)

Categorisation

When deciding which categories will be used in order to collate data for analysis, it is important to remember that as the number of categories is reduced the loss of information increases.

Using the example of our sample of forty social workers in our examination of their caseload size according to age, we could use the following categories for the presentation of our findings in frequency or contingency tables and for statistical analysis (Table 3.1).

It is immediately apparent that if there was a pure chance distribution for each contingency, the numbers in each cell would be so small ($40 \div 4$ cells $\times$ 4 cells $= 16 = 2.5$ per cell) as to make a meaningful statistical analysis impossible.

It is also apparent that by so categorising our data we may have lost some vital information. For example, if we observed that for the 45+ year old group there were ten social workers with caseloads of fewer

TABLE 3.1. SOCIAL WORKER'S CASELOAD ACCORDING TO AGE OF SOCIAL WORKER

Caseload size	25 years	25–34 years	35–44 years	Over 45 years	Total
Less than 20 cases 20–29 cases 30–39 cases Over 40 cases					
Total					

than twenty clients, we could have hidden the real finding that all ten were over 60 years old. If, because the number of people in the sample were too small to apply the selected test, we combined the age groups so that only two remained (i.e. under 35 years and over 35 years) we would lose even more information and this would be further compounded if we also reduced the number of categories for caseload size.

In addition to considering categorisation in relation to sample size and statistical analysis, the four basic rules given in Chapter 2 should be generally observed (page 15). Another important consideration in the design stage is the *reliability* and *validity* of any measures used. Reliability, according to Moser (1958), is ". . . the extent to which repeated measurements made on the same material, by the same measuring instrument, would get the same result . . ." whilst validity is the extent of the accuracy of a specific measure in measuring what it is purported to measure.

Data Collection

THE QUESTIONNAIRE

One of the most frequent methods of data collection in the social sciences is that of the questionnaire. It comprises a list of questions which are open-ended (allowing the respondent freedom in the manner in which he answers the question) or a list of questions with a limited list of alternative replies prepared in accordance with some predetermined criteria. The questionnaire can be completed either by the respondent himself, thus making it an appropriate instrument for submission through the post, or by the researcher (or his agent) as he puts questions to the respondent.

The decision to use a questionnaire or other instrument for data collection stems from the study design and the nature of the enquiry. The following questions, however, are pertinent to the decision.

1. Do the data required necessitate the use of methods of observation in order that they might be accurately obtained?
2. Are the data required such that only disguised tests are likely to be successful?
3. Are the data of such a personal or embarrassing nature that only a skilful interviewer is likely to obtain them?
4. Is the quantity of data required from each respondent such that only a small response could be anticipated in the absence of face to face contact?
5. Is current knowledge in the proposed area of research so limited that it is not possible to formulate the questions adequately and that further "exploratory" interviews are required?
6. Are the data required such as to necessitate personal contact in order to explain their value or assure their treatment in accordance with high ethical standards?
7. Is the nature of the data required such that it would be unlikely to provoke any interest or enthusiasm on the part of the recipient?

If these questions do not yield any affirmative response (and whether they do or not is often evaluation of a skilful judgement), then it is likely that a questionnaire can be the main means of data collection.

Should this be so then some very real gains will accrue to this particular method.

1. The questionnaire can be submitted to respondents through the post thus reaching large numbers of respondents at negligible costs relative to interview and travelling costs and making it easier to cover a large geographical area.
2. Researcher time is substantially reduced when no interview is required.

3. The questionnaire can be developed, discussed and tested more thoroughly than almost all other forms of data collection.
4. The standardisation of the questionnaire can ensure greater uniformity.
5. The respondent can place greater confidence in the anonymity of the questionnaire.
6. Questionnaires place less pressure upon the respondent to give an immediate response.

All forms of data collection have disadvantages and the postal questionnaire is no exception. Its drawbacks may include the following:

1. Not all respondents are able to read.
2. All respondents will not have a similar grasp of the content of the questionnaire.
3. It is possible to ensure that the questions are fully understood by the majority of its recipients, but it is not always possible to detect the answers to misunderstood questions or the possibility of the respondent giving inaccurate data.
4. The response rate to the questionnaire is inevitably lower than that to the well-conducted personal interview.
5. Nothing can be done about questions that are unanswered or only partially answered.

The response rate to a questionnaire will be influenced by:

1. The status and/or authority of the sender.
2. The layout, attractiveness and simplicity of the questionnaire.
3. The section or letter of explanation of the study, the ethics of it and the appeal made to the respondent.
4. The length of the questionnaire.
5. The ease with which the questionnaire can be completed.
6. The characteristics and commitment of the people to whom the questionnaire is sent.
7. The ease of returning the completed questionnaire, and the inducement to do so.
8. The ascertainment of the location of the desired respondents.
9. The intricacy of the steps which have to be taken to contact the proposed recipients.
10. The timing.

It must never be assumed that the non-responders are a "like" group to the responders, though it is often possible to show similarities of certain variables, e.g. Age/Sex/Social Class, etc.

Construction of the questionnaire must be addressed directly to the problem which the researcher proposes to investigate. A questionnaire cannot be a substitute for a vague or inadequately formulated problem, nor can it compensate for any defects in the research design.

If we conclude that the questionnaire is the most appropriate data-gathering technique, then in its construction we will need to ensure that the questions will initiate responses that are acceptable indicators of those variables that we wish to study, i.e. that they are operationally satisfactory. For example, we may wish to study the values held by newly qualified social workers of their clients. Values themselves cannot be seen, and it is not considered practicable to "sit-in" with social workers over a long period of time in order to assess the values held. An operational approach would be to ask questions such as, "Should social workers be willing to give up some of their leisure time in order to meet the urgent needs of a client?" A response in the affirmative (subject to suitable testing for validity and reliability) would be taken as an indication of the value of high commitment to clients.

The questionnaire, like the interview but unlike observation and disguised tests, presupposes that most people tell most of the truth most of the time. This is a limitation, yet one that is common to all human activity, for society itself rests upon this assumption. It does stress the need to ensure that all advantages accruing to being untruthful are removed and that there are no disadvantages to being completely frank. A saving factor is that the questionnaire is used in quantitative research and the better the response rate the less the deviant response will influence the final result.

Each question should gather information on a specific aspect of the study or to test the accuracy of responses to other questions. The presence of each question needs to be justified. Once it has been decided to use a questionnaire and requisite questions formulated it is tempting to add additional questions beyond those originally intended on the grounds that the extra data would be interesting and that no extra cost would be involved. The "extra" should only be included after a very careful evaluation of their likely contribution to the basic study. Additional questions are likely to reduce the response rate and would also involve extra cost, if not in collection, then certainly in tabulation, calculation, analysis and interpretation. One permitted exception would be an open-ended question such as, "Any further comments?"

As many questions as possible should be pre-coded with fixed replies. This makes the handling of the data much easier and should ensure a relevant response to the question. One danger to the pre-coded question is that it might initiate a response that would not otherwise have been given. It can, however, be argued that nothing meaningful can be said about human beings or human activity without categorisation and that categorisation necessarily involves minor inaccuracies. Discussion with colleagues and a well-planned study should do much to ensure that pre-coded answers are not misleading or emotive and are pertinent to the question.

Such are the advantages of pre-coding that open-ended questions should only be used if well justified. Adequate justification would include:

1. That the extent of existing knowledge is such that it is not possible or practicable to pre-code the reply.
2. Where the data from an open-ended supplementary question will serve as a check on the accuracy of a pre-coded question.
3. Where the data will descriptively enrich the response to a pre-coded question.
4. Where by giving pre-coded response it is likely that there will be bias in the response given (e.g. it is better to ask, "What social work journals do you read regularly?" than to say, "Please examine this list of social work journals and tick the ones which you read regularly", if an accurate response is required).

If a research project calls for the use of interviewers in the completion of questionnaires it is of extreme importance that the interviewers are briefed adequately so that the questionnaire will be introduced in a uniform manner. It is wise to prepare a written guide for each interviewer to ensure this.

The guide should be comprehensive and its preamble should state clearly the importance of the interviewer knowing the questionnaire thoroughly, of adhering to the guide and of accurate and complete recording. Guidance should be given to cover the following areas.

(i) *The presentation of the project to the respondent.* This should include instructions about putting the respondent at ease; explanation as to how and why the respondent was selected; establishing the authority of the interviewer; and the importance of the interviewer being alert and organised.

(ii) *The conduct of the interview.* This should include instructions which will prevent the interviewer from influencing the respondent's views, anticipating responses, will guard against assumptions and will ensure that all responses are checked before they are recorded.

(iii) *Probing and prompting.* It is permissible to probe matters of fact, but the interviewer should be made aware that matters of opinion are very sensitive to suggestion. Interviewers should be instructed that they must not paraphrase questions and if asked the meaning of a question, that they should indicate what is wanted is the respondent's reaction to it—what it means to him.

(iv) *Recording replies.* The questionnaire should be so arranged that most of the replies are to be recorded with scrupulous accuracy, *at the time they are given.*
Only a good knowledge of the questionnaire will allow the interviewer to concentrate on what the informant is saying and to get the exact meaning of each reply. Before completing the interview the interviewer should be asked to check that all the questions have been asked and that *all* other necessary information has been recorded.

Data Collation

It is inevitable that consideration of data processing is related to the construction of questionnaires as well as to those of data analysis. There is little point in posing questions which cannot subsequently be analysed nor can we prepare contingency tables for categories of response which have not been allowed for in the design stage. In gathering together the information collected we must have considered previously what we want to do with the data and whether or not the variables and their categories used will test the hypotheses outlined in the problem formulation stage (page 28).

It is of great help in correctly anticipating the coding of a data-gathering instrument to decide upon the data-collation instrument at the same time. Such an instrument can be as simple as a paper and pencil tally sheet, but since in most research we are concerned to combine categories of one variable with categories of several others, it is usually necessary to use some method of collation which will permit cross-sorting.

The simplest data-collation instrument which will permit this is the edge-punched card. Ideally these are used only for small numbers of respondents and comparatively short questionnaires. These cards have numbered holes punched along the edges. These numbered holes are allocated to the questions which have been posed and for any particular response the hole is opened by the use of clippers. When all the data have been transferred from the data collection instrument these cards can then be sorted by placing a needle through any hole number desired. Only these cards which have been "clipped" will fall off, leaving the unclipped records on the needle. We could, for example, have a hole for the sex of the respondent and a series of holes allocated to age. If we put the needle through the hole which had been cut for "female" the sexes of the respondents would separate out. Keeping the cards separate for sex we would then "needle" each category of age and by counting these separately for males and females a frequency table could be created. By using permutations of hole allocation it is possible to have a considerable amount of data of each card.

When the number of respondents exceeds 300 it then becomes necessary to use other types of cards which are machine punched and sorted by tabulators or computers. If this method is being used it is advisable to consult members of a computer department. They should be involved *before* questionnaires are administered so that appropriate coding can be agreed to ensure that there will be no difficulties met in the subsequent tabulations and data analysis.

Using either system it must be realised that in transferring data from the collection instrument to the collation one there can be error and great care must be taken to ensure that this is kept to an absolute minimum by checking and rechecking.

We would emphasise what we pointed out at the beginning, this chapter covers only sufficient information to help the reader to understand what is involved in the research process and we would recommend further reading, as listed, before embarking on a specific research project.

In conclusion we present a brief summary of the whole process of social work research from the problem formulation to the preparation of the report in order to see the various steps in context.

I. PROBLEM FORMULATION

    A. Is the research problem relevant to social work and, if so, how?

    B. Is the conceptualisation appropriate and adequate?

        1. Are relevant concepts defined?

        2. Are the hypotheses clear and researchable?

        3. Are the hypotheses justified by a review of prior knowledge relating to them?

        4. If there is a theory, is it parsimonious and logically consistent?

    C. Is the problem specified in researchable terms? Are the connections between concepts and the research operations clear and specific?

    D. Is the statement of the problem based upon an adequate rationale in terms of related theory and research?

II. THE DATA-GATHERING DESIGN

    A. Does the design for gathering data relate to the problem and objectives of the study?

    B. Are the data suitable to make operational the variable(s) sought?

    C. Are relevant variables controlled by the design?

    D. Is the sampling of subjects appropriate?

    E. Is the sample of variables appropriate?

    F. Is the sample of situations or practice contexts appropriate?

    G. Is the design repeatable?

III. DATA-GATHERING TECHNIQUES

    A. Are the techniques for gathering data adequate in range and appropriateness?

    B. Are the techniques for gathering data clearly a means by which variables of the study may be made operational?

    C. Are problems of reliability addressed and, if so, how?

    D. Are problems of validity addressed and, if so, how?

    E. Are types of instrument error taken into account, and, if so, how?

    F. Are the procedures associated with data-gathering repeatable?

IV. DATA-PROCESSING TECHNIQUES

    A. Are the data-classifying techniques adequate and clear?

    B. Are the data-combining techniques adequate and clear?

    C. Are the data-describing techniques adequate and clear?

    D. Are the data-relating techniques adequate and clear?

V. INTERPRETATION OF DATA AND RESULTS

    A. Is the logic of inference correct in relationship to such factors as the following:

        1. The extent to which the conclusions on the study are warranted by the logic of the design, the techniques employed and the means for processing data?

        2. The degree to which the generalisations from the study to populations of persons, variables, methods and situations are warranted by the design, data-gathering techniques and data-processing techniques?

    B. If there are theoretical implications of the study, are these drawn out and, if so, in what fashion?

    C. If there are practical implications of the results, are these explained and, if so, in what manner?

VI. THE REPORT

A. Is the writing clear?
B. Is the writing succinct?
C. Is there proper documentation?
D. Is the report complete?
E. Are the findings discussed properly in relationship to the presentation of data?
F. Are the findings presented clearly and logically in relationship to the design and research problem?
G. Is the exposition of the study presented logically so as to communicate effectively to the reader?

References

MOSER, C. A. (1958) *Survey Methods in Social Investigation*. London: Heinemann.
WEISS, R. S. (1968) *Statistics in Social Research: an Introduction*. New York: Wiley.

Recommended Reading

BETTLEHEIM, B. (1950) *Love is Not Enough*. Glencoe, Illinois: The Free Press.
PARSLOE, P. (1965) Presenting reality—the choice of a casework method. *Brit. J. Psychiat. Soc. Wk.* **8**, 1.
POLANSKY, N. A., DESAIX, C. and SHARLIN, S. A. (1972) *Child Neglect: Understanding and Reaching the Parent*. New York: Child Welfare League of America.
REINER, B. S. and KAUFMAN, I. (1959) *Character Disorders in Parents of Delinquents*. New York: Family Service Association of America.
TURNER, F. J. (Ed.) (1968) *Differential Diagnosis and Treatment in Social Work*. New York: Free Press.

CHAPTER 4

Sources of Information in Applied Social Studies*

THIS chapter outlines some of the categories of publications within the area of applied social studies which are at present available for all who need them. The problem of unpublished information—correspondence, statistical data, case books, histories and interviews—awaits separate treatment. The chapter concludes with a description of the sequence of steps which should be undertaken by anyone seeking to discover what is the present state of knowledge within a particular topic.

Guides to the Literature of the Social Sciences and Psychology

With the great rise in research activity, notably during the present century, the literature of all subjects has increased tremendously. The growth rate has been shown to be exponential, and in some areas of social work leads to a doubling of the available literature twice in a decade! As it grows, it becomes more complex. Because few subjects are now restricted by national boundaries, an awareness of what has been published in other countries is necessary. Introductory guides to the literature of certain subjects—notably some scientific ones—have been available for a considerable time, but in recent years such guides have been published on many topics for the first time. Many of these are separately published as books; some are produced by librarians, whilst others are the work of practitioners in their own fields. Apart from those separately published, brief guides appear from time to time in the professional journals. They usually cover a wide range of

* This chapter was contributed by C. A. Crossley, a librarian at the University of Bradford.

sources of information within a subject, including notes on relevant libraries, societies, periodicals, indexes and abstracts, handbooks, reviews, data books, bibliographies, standard books, encyclopaedias and dictionaries, theses, biographical information, research associations, as appropriate. The following have relevance in the various areas of the social sciences.

(i)   *Literature of the Social Sciences*, by P. R. Lewis (London, Library Association, 1960).

(ii)   *Sources of Information in the Social Sciences*, by Carl M. White (New Jersey, Bedminster Press, 1964).
This book has annotated bibliographies at the end of each chapter.

(iii)   *Reader's Guide to the Social Sciences*, by B. F. Hoselitz (New York, Free Press; rev. ed. London, Collier–Macmillan, 1970).

(iv)   *Research Materials in the Social Sciences*, by J. A. Clarke (2nd ed. Madison, Wis., University of Wisconsin Press, 1967).

(v)   *Guide to Unpublished Research Materials*, edited by R. Staveley (London, Library Association, 1957).
W. L. Guttsman surveys the problem of unpublished information in a chapter entitled "Materials and sources in sociology", whilst another chapter, by C. M. Franks, covers similar materials in psychology.
Barbara Kyle's chapter "Towards bibliographical control of unpublished material" contains a list of guides which is itself still useful.

(vi)   *Reference Books in the Social Sciences and Humanities*, by R. E. Stevens (Champaign, Ill., Illini Union Bookstore, 1966).

(vii)   *A Guide to the Documentation of Psychology*, by C. K. Elliott (London, Clive Bingley, 1971).

(viii)   *How to Find Out in Philosophy and Psychology*, by D. H. Borchardt (London, Pergamon, 1968).

General Bibliographies and Catalogues

It should hardly be necessary to remind a research worker to use his own library catalogue, but, because so few have received formal and systematic instruction in its use, many people are unable to take advantage of its resources. All libraries should possess a detailed subject catalogue as complement to the author section. The subject catalogue may take the form of entries under the subject headings arranged alphabetically, or a classified catalogue may be provided. The latter reflects exactly the order of the books on the shelf and always requires approach via an alphabetical subject index. The collection of entries in this index under each heading reveals how various aspects of a subject may be scattered throughout a library and similar help is provided in the alphabetical subject catalogue by following up the cross-references given.

To record the output of published books and, in certain cases, other documents, trade bibliographies exist in many countries. In recent years there has been an encouraging increase in the number of national bibliographies produced by official organisations which list books and publications even more authoritatively and often with fuller details. English-language material is covered by many such works. Publications which fall into this category are:

(i) *Bookseller* (London, Whitaker). A weekly publication with monthly cumulations which, in combination with the same firm's *Books of the Month and Books to Come*, eventually appear quarterly as:

(ii) *Cumulative Book List* (London, Whitaker). This list has a yearly volume and cumulations covering four- or five-year periods.

(iii) *British Books* (London, Publishers' Circular). A monthly publication which appears in annual form as:

(iv) *English Catalogue of Books* (London, Publishers' Circular). There are five-yearly cumulations and use of these allows for retrospective searching back to the beginning of the nineteenth century.

(v) *British Books in Print* (London, Whitaker). Annual list of over 250,000 books currently available on sale, listed separately by authors and by titles.

(vi) *British National Bibliography* (London, Council of B.N.B.). Since 1950 this has been the best source of full information about new British publications. It appears weekly and has cumulations quarterly, yearly and five-yearly, with appropriate author, title and subject indexes. Its classified arrangement permits subject searches to be made most effectively.

(vii)   *Cumulative Book Index* (New York, Wilson). Appears monthly with cumulations covering up to two years or more. Aims to include all English-language material, but emphasis is on North American publications. With its predecessor, *United States Catalog*, provides complete twentieth-century coverage.

(viii) *Books in Print* (New York, Bowker). The United States equivalent of (v) above, with separate volumes for authors and titles.

(ix)   *Subject Guide to Books in Print* (New York, Bowker). A companion to (viii), rearranging the publications under subject headings.

All library catalogues are useful. Those of major collections, particularly national libraries and those known to specialise in one subject field, are especially valuable. Catalogues of note include the following:

(i)   *General Catalogue of Printed Books* (British Museum). The complete catalogue is now available in approximately 260 volumes up to the year 1955, with multi-volume supplements for later years. This is an author catalogue; subject approach to the collection has to be made via the *Subject Index Volumes* which each cover five-year periods. The *Subject Index* last published relates to the quinquennium 1956–60.

(ii)   *The National Union Catalog.* This provides a guide to the library holdings of all the major institutions of the United States. It is compiled by the Library of Congress, Washington, D.C., and grew out of the catalogue of that library, which is itself much larger than the British Museum Library. Backed be generous funds and imaginative law, Congress and other libraries acquire materials on the grand scale. The Library of Congress *Catalog* has two sections: authors and subjects. The arrangement under subjects is very much more specific than the equivalent in the British Museum *Subject Index* and is outstandingly helpful in searches. The *National Union Catalog* also will eventually have a separate subject section.

(iii) *The London Bibliography of the Social Sciences.* The several volumes of this work record additions to the library of the London School of Economics over different periods of its history and the subject arrangement of the volumes makes them eminently suitable for subject approach. The Seventh Supplement (Vols. XXII–XXVIII) brings the catalogue up to the end of 1972.

(iv) *U.S. Department of Health, Education and Welfare. Library Catalog.* The catalogue of this important library is published by the American firm of G. K. Hall in a set of volumes wherein the entries are reproduced by offset photolithography, thereby constituting a major bibliography with first-rate coverage of United States official publications.

(v) International Organisations. Printed catalogues of the publications in the libraries of the United Nations and World Health Organisation are also available and are up-dated from time to time.

Bibliographies

The initial aim of the research worker is to produce a list of references on his topic and it is possible that such a list has already been compiled. If it has been published he need only acquire it and bring it up-to-date by the use of later sources. The first task is to identify that one has indeed been published. The researcher requires, then, a list of such lists, i.e. a bibliography of bibliographies.

(i) *Bibliography of Bibliographies* (4th and final edition), by Theodore Besterman (4 vols., Lausanne, Societas Bibliographica, 1965–6). This covers 117,000 separate bibliographies on all subjects published in all periods and in all languages. Works are listed alphabetically by subject. It has two main limitations:
(a) It covers only separately published bibliographies.
(b) It will increasingly become out-of-date.

(ii)   *Bibliographic Index* (New York, H. W. Wilson Company).
       This is a continuing service which has appeared regularly
       since 1938. It is published half-yearly and cumulates into
       yearly or multi-annual volumes. Works are listed alpha-
       betically by subject and include bibliographies which appear
       in books and also those which form part of a periodical.

There are many excellent bibliographies published in the fields of social
work and psychology. Many contain brief annotations for each item
listed. Amongst them may be numbered:

(iii) *The Handicapped Child*, by R. Dinnage (London, Longmans,
       1970).
(iv)   *Probation Since World War II*, by D. C. Tompkins (Berkeley,
       Calif., Institute of Government Studies, University of Cali-
       fornia, 1964).
(v)   *Aging in the Modern World*, U.S. Office of Aging (Washing-
       ton, U.S. Department of Health, Education and Welfare,
       1963).
(vi)   *Home and School Relationships*, by E. Goodacre (London,
       Home and School Council, 1968).

More general bibliographies include:

(vii) *More Books on the Social Services* (London, National Council
       of Social Services, 1973).
(viii) *Bibliography of Social Work and Administration, 1930–1953*,
       by P. M. Birkett (London, Joint University Council for Social
       and Public Administration, 1954. Plus supplements).
(ix)   *Classified Bibliography for the Field of Social Work* (Santa
       Clara, Calif., Premier Publications, 1959). Lists 5500 books,
       articles, government publications, dissertations and AV
       materials on counselling, guidance and social work.
(x)   *Index of Psychoanalytical Writings*, by A. Grinstein (5 vols.,
       New York, International Universities Press, 1956–60).
       Covers the entire output from 1896 to 1960 in this branch of
       psychology.
(xi)   *Guide to Psychiatric Books*, by K. A. Menninger (2nd rev. ed.,
       New York, Grune & Stratton, 1956).

(xii)   *Harvard List of Books in Psychology* (4th ed., Cambridge, Mass., Harvard U.P., 1971).

Information about new publications may be obtained from:

(xiii)   *Recent Publications in the Social and Behavioral Sciences; the ABS Guide* (American Behavioral Scientist, Annual supplements).

Guides to Research

Much research activity is carried out in institutions of higher education of one kind or another and this frequently culminates in a Master's degree or a Ph.D. The theses on which these awards are based are usually deposited in the library of the university concerned. They normally contain much original thought and report work at a high level. Because of this these sources of information cannot be ignored and they may be located nowadays by several means:

(i)   *Aslib Index of Theses Accepted for Higher Degrees in the Universities of Great Britain and Ireland* (London, Aslib, 1950–1). An annual publication which lists each year's output under subject headings such as sociology and social psychology. For each thesis the name of the author, the title, the degree and the university or college concerned are indicated. A subject index to each volume gives more specific access.

(ii)   *Dissertation Abstracts International* (Ann Arbor, Michigan, University Microfilms, 1938–). A very much fuller service giving more satisfactory information at more frequent intervals. Appears monthly in two parts: Part A deals with social sciences and humanities, whilst Part B covers the sciences and engineering (this section includes psychology). For each thesis a lengthy descriptive summary is given, in addition to details of author, title, institution, etc. A detailed subject index, which cumulates yearly, makes access even more effective; a yearly author index allows for approach by name. Coverage is limited to doctoral theses. In 1970 a

Retrospective Index was published in eight subject volumes of computer-compiled indexes and one volume of author index. Volume IV contains psychology, sociology and political science, and includes social work. Volume VIII, in two parts, covers education.

(iii) *Master's Abstracts* (Ann Arbor, Michigan, University Microfilms, 1962–). Covers Masters' theses of American universities and colleges.

(iv) *Research Studies in Education* (Bloomington, Ind., Phi Delta Kappan, Inc.). An occasional bibliography of American doctoral dissertations, reports and field studies. First published 1952. Later editions cover 1953–63 and 1963–7, with subsequent annual listings.

(v) *A Select List of Research, Surveys and Theses in Youth Work, Adolescence and Allied Educational and Social Fields, 1960–1968* (Leicester, National College for the Training of Youth Leaders, 1969).

Such listings may also be located by *Bibliographic Index* (see under Bibliographies (ii)), where they are entered in a section headed "Dissertations", in addition to an extra entry under the name of the subject itself.

(vi) *Social Service Review*. Social work dissertations (with abstracts) have been listed since 1954.

(vii) *Smith College Studies in Social Work*. Lists Smith College theses (with abstracts) annually.

News of current academic research is contained, for Britain, in:

(viii) *Scientific Research in British Universities and Colleges* (3 vols., London, H.M.S.O., Annual). Volume 3 of this publication covers the social sciences and lists by subject headings such as "Social administration", "Sociology", all current research activities for each institution, arranged alphabetically by name of university.

(ix) *Register of Research Projects in the Social Sciences in Progress in Ireland* (Dublin, Economic and Social Research Institute, 1973–).

(x)   *Register of Research into Higher Education in Western Europe* (Society for Research into Higher Education, 1968–   ).

(xi) *Current Researches in Education and Educational Psychology* (Slough, National Foundation for Educational Research in England and Wales, 1960–   ).

(xii) *Old Age: a Register of Social Research, 1972 onwards* (London, National Corporation for the Care of Old People, 1973–   ). First published in 1964 and updated with annual supplements. Now loose-leaf binder format.

Guides to American research include:

(xiii) *Research in Education* (Education Resources Information Center, 1966–   ).

(xiv) *Research relating to Children* (Washington, U.S. Children's Bureau, 1948–9).

(xv) *Research relating to Juvenile Delinquents* (Washington, U.S. Children's Bureau, 1962–   ).

(xvi) *Research relating to Mentally Retarded Children* (Washington, U.S. Children's Bureau, 1960–   ).

(xvii) *Current Sociological Research* (New York, American Sociological Association, 1953–   ).

All these formal guides supplement the information which is often given regularly in professional journals.

Review Series

Reviews constitute an important source of information. They take the form of periodic surveys of progress in specific subjects and sometimes cover several years' work and development, though in some subjects they are limited to annual surveys. They are normally prepared by an authority on the subject in question; are usually comprehensive in coverage, paying due regard to foreign work and publications; frequently provide a synopsis, tabulated to show coverage of each review and almost always contain a lengthy bibliography of recent publications. Many now appear in book form, frequently annually, with titles like, "Annual Review of . . .", "Advances in . . .", "Progress in . . .". Examples of these include:

(i) *Advances in Child Development and Behavior* (New York, Academic Press, Vol. 1, 1963–).

(ii) *Advances in Experimental Social Psychology* (New York, Academic Press, Vol. 1, 1964–).

(iii) *Annual Progress in Child Psychiatry and Child Development* (New York, Brunner; London, Butterworths, Vol. 1, 1968–).

(iv) *Annual Review of Psychology* (Stanford, California, Annual Review Inc., Vol. 1, 1950–).

(v) *Annual Survey of Psychoanalysis* (New York, International Universities Press, Vols. 1–5, 1950–4).

(vi) *Progress in Psychotherapy* (New York, Grune & Stratton, Vols. 1–5, 1956–60).

(vii) *Psychoanalytic Study of the Child* (London, Hogarth Press, Vol. 1, 1945–).

(viii) *Year Book of Psychiatry and Applied Mental Health* (Chicago, Year Book Medical Publishers, Inc., 1970–).

(ix) *Encyclopaedia of Social Work*, edited by H. L. Luric (New York, National Association of Social Workers, 1965–). This was previously published under the title *Social Work Yearbook*, 1920–60.

Other reviews are published in the normal periodical literature; for example:

(x) *American Journal of Psychiatry.*
(xi) *Psychological Bulletin.*

Encyclopaedias and Dictionaries

Encyclopaedias and dictionaries range from the general and popular to the very specialised and highly professional, but all may have their uses. Even a general work provides an introduction to a subject with which one is not completely familiar and will provide a state-of-the-art survey, with recommended reading for further information. From such an article one can learn the names of prominent workers in the field and can discover the terminology of the subject, which helps to provide entry points into the specialised indexing and abstract services. Examples under this heading include:

   (i)   *Encyclopaedia Britannica* (Chicago, Encyclopaedia Britannica, Inc.).
   (ii) *Chambers' Encyclopaedia* (London, Pergamon Press, 1966).

In addition to these general encyclopaedias, there are:

   (iii) *Encyclopaedia of the Social Sciences* (London, Macmillan, 1952). This is a 15-volume work first published in the years 1930–5, but much of the material in it is still of relevance, and this accounts for its reprinting.

A new work of comparable size is:

   (iv) *International Encyclopaedia of the Social Sciences* (17 vols., New York, Macmillan, 1968). Lengthy, signed articles are a feature of this work; the user will find adequate bibliographies appended to each.
   (v)   *Encyclopaedia of Education* (10 vols., New York, Macmillan and Free Press, 1971).

Less formidable undertakings include:

   (vi) *Encyclopaedia of Child Care and Guidance*, edited by S. M. Gruenberg (New York, Doubleday, 1954).
   (vii) *Encyclopaedia of Educational Research*, by R. L. Ebel (4th ed., New York, Macmillan, 1969).
   (viii) *Blond's Encyclopedia of Education*, edited by E. Blishen (London, Blond, 1969).

The research worker in social sciences has choice of a wide range of dictionaries, from the popular to the specialist:

   (ix) *Dictionary of Psychology*, by J. Drever (rev. ed., Harmondsworth, Penguin Books, 1964).
   (x)   *Comprehensive Dictionary of Psychological and Psychoanalytical Terms*, by H. B. and A. C. English (London, Longmans, 1958). Defines about 9600 terms.
   (xi) *Dictionary of Psychology*, by H. C. Warren (London, Allen & Unwin, 1935). This is an older publication but is still useful.

Contains about 8000 terms. Gives many French and German equivalents.

(xii)   *Psychiatric Dictionary*, by L. E. Hinsie and R. J. Campbell (3rd ed., New York, Oxford University Press, 1960).

(xiii)   *Dictionary of the Social Sciences*, edited by J. Gould and W. L. Kolb (London, Tavistock Publications, 1964).

(xiv)   *Dictionary of Social Science*, by J. T. Zadrozny (Washington, Public Affairs Press, 1958).

(xv)   *Dictionary of Sociology*, by G. D. Mitchell (London, Routledge, 1968). Presents definitions, illustrations, and a history of the use of the words it includes, in addition to many articles of considerable length.

(xvi)   *Dictionary of Social Services: Policy and Practice*, compiled by J. Clegg (National Council for Social Service Press, 1971).

(xvii)   *Glossary of Social Work Terms in English–French–German*, by A. Lorenzi (Cologne, Haymanns Verlag, 1956). The function of this dictionary is translation rather than definition.

(xviii)   *Dictionary of Education*, by C. V. Good (2nd ed., New York, McGraw-Hill, 1959).

Handbooks

The research worker who needs data of various kinds (excluding statistics for the moment) or information about experimental methods will often find that a compilation of relevant material has already been produced. Examples of these are:

(i)   *Handbook of Experimental Psychology*, edited by S. S. Stevens (New York, Wiley, 1951).

(ii)   *Mental Measurements Yearbook*, edited by O. K. Buros (Highland Park, N. Jersey, Gryphon). This is a series which first appeared in 1935 under the title *Educational, Psychological and Personality Tests of 1933 and 1934*. The seventh Yearbook was published in two volumes in 1972.

(iii)   *Handbook of Research Methods in Child Development*, edited by P. H. Mussen (New York, Wiley, 1960).

(iv)   *American Handbook of Psychiatry*, edited by S. Arieti (2 vols., New York, Basic Books Inc., 1959; reprinted 1962–4).

(v) *Manual of Child Psychology*, edited by L. Carmichael (New York, Wiley, 1954).

Conferences and Symposia

Conferences and symposia, particularly international meetings, are not rated highly enough as media for the transmission of new ideas in many subjects. Hundreds take place each year. For the benefit of those who cannot be present, the proceedings are frequently published in one form or another. These proceedings frequently include the discussion which follows presentation of a paper, as well as the full text of the paper itself. Two problems create difficulties for the non-participant who seeks to benefit from the information circulated.

One concerns the announcement that a conference will take place, giving details of the content, the speakers, their papers, and the location and date. Several services now exist solely to announce forthcoming meetings. Amongst these can be numbered:

Selected list of Scientific Meetings to be held during . . . (Month, year).
Naval Scientific and Technical Information Centre
(St. Mary Cray, Kent, Ministry of Defence).

Forthcoming International Scientific and Technical Conferences,
Aslib (London, Aslib).

Scientific Meetings.
Special Libraries Association
(New York, Special Libraries Association).

World List of Future International Meetings.
United States. Library of Congress
(Washington, D.C., Library of Congress).
Part 2 covers social, cultural, humanistic and commercial fields.

Technical Meetings Index.
Technical Meetings Information Service
(New Hartford, N.Y., 1964–   ).
Union of International Associations.

Annual International Congress Calendar.
(Brussels, U.I.A.).
(Kept up to date monthly in *International Associations.*)

World Meetings: United States and Canada
(New York, Macmillan Information).

World Meetings: Outside United States and Canada
(New York, Macmillan Information).

Many periodicals include announcements of forthcoming conferences in their news sections and, in particular, most learned societies and professional bodies announce in their journals conferences which they themselves organise or meetings of interest to their members organised by any other body.

The second problem regarding conferences relates to reports of the meetings and publication of the proceedings. Many periodicals give brief reports on recently held meetings which concern their readers and often given an indication of any intention to publish the proceedings. A few commercial publishers specialise in publishing proceedings of such conferences. Notable examples in Britain are Pergamon and Butterworth, and catalogues issued by such publishers should be checked for information. Some learned societies sponsor conferences and subsequently publish the resulting papers. They are frequently published in named series and are comparatively easy to trace in catalogues of publishers or libraries, or in trade bibliographies such as the *British National Bibliography.*

There are several regular publications which give details of published proceedings and a few large, infrequent bibliographies contain such information. Examples of these are:

(i)   *Directory of Published Proceedings* (Harrison, N.Y., InterDok Corp.).
      Published in two series: SSH (Social Sciences and Humanities), quarterly, and SEMT (Science, Engineering, Medicine and Technology), monthly (10 per year). Cumulated indexes annually.

(ii) *Index of Conference Proceedings received by the BLL* (Boston Spa, Yorks., British Library Lending Division). Published monthly. Cumulated subject keyword index in December issue.

(iii) *Proceedings in Print* (Mattapan, Mass., Proceedings in Print Inc.).

Published bi-monthly. Contains single combined index of subject keywords, sponsoring bodies, editors, etc., cumulated in December issue.

Guides published at longer intervals include:

(iv) *Yearbook of International Congress Proceedings* (Brussels, Union of International Associations, 1969–   ).

First edition, published 1969, covered proceedings of meetings held between 1960 and 1969; second edition, 1970, listed proceedings of meetings held 1962 to 1969. Bi-annual publication, covering preceding 8 years, is planned. This series superseded *Bibliography of Proceedings of International Meetings*, itself an annual cumulation of a monthly: *Bibliographical Current List of Papers, Reports, and Proceedings of International Meetings*, which was published between 1960 and 1968.

Proceedings of older conferences may also be located through specially-compiled bibliographies; the following is one example:

(v) *International Congresses and Conferences*, 1840–1937, compiled by Winifred Gregory (New York, Wilson, 1938).

In addition, certain of the major abstracting services offer access to information on conferences in their fields of interest. For instance, *Psychological Abstracts* provides a heading in its subject indexes under the word "Symposium" under which to record such publications. (In the monthly Brief Subject Indexes for 1973 this was altered to "Professional Meetings and Symposia".)

Locating a paper known to have been presented at a conference depends on its inclusion in an abstracts journal, when it can be traced via its author or subject. Such inclusion normally involves considerable delay, of course, but there is no one service which aims to give access to individual papers in a systematic and timely fashion. *Current Index to Conference Papers* gave brief hope, but survived only two years.

Government Publications

All branches of the social sciences are of concern to governments, at all levels from local, through national, to international. Official activity includes research, enquiry, legislation, survey and statistics collection. All such activity results in publication and provides thereby a rich field of knowledge. Information about their publications is obtainable from their many catalogues. These range—in Britain—from a *Daily List*, through monthly catalogues to annual cumulations. Arrangement in such catalogues is frequently—as in Britain—by issuing Ministry or Department, but subject access is almost always possible via indexes to the catalogues themselves. In Britain and the United States, for example, the monthly and annual catalogues provide such access. Five-year indexes are also available for British government publications. The more important documents also feature in the national bibliographies such as *British National Bibliography*.

International organisations such as United Nations, Unesco, World Health Organisation, also produce many publications of potential interest. Current information about them is available through the Daily Lists and annual catalogues issued by H.M.S.O. in Britain. Besides such sources of information, the individual organisations publish catalogues of their output from time to time; the following are examples:

(i)   *Ten Years of United Nations Publications, 1945–1955* (New York, United Nations, 1955).

(ii) *Publications . . . 1958–1962* (World Health Organisation, 1964).

For more than casual use of such official publications the research worker is recommended to consult one or more of several excellent guides:

(iii) *An Introduction to British Government Publications*, by J. G. Ollé (2nd ed., London, Association of Assistant Librarians, 1973).

(iv) *A Guide to Parliamentary Papers*, by P. and G. Ford (London, Blackwell, 1955).

(v)   *Government Information and the Research Worker*, by R.

Staveley and M. Piggott (2nd ed., London, Library Association, 1965).

(vi) *British Official Publications*, by J. E. Pemberton (2nd ed., London, Pergamon, 1973).

U.S. government publications are covered by:

(vii) *Government Publications and their Use*, by L. F. Schmeckebier and R. B. Eastin (rev. ed., Washington, D.C., Brookings Institution, 1969).

(viii) *Research Resources: Annotated Guide to the Social Sciences*, Vol. 2, *Official Publications*, by J. B. Mason (Santa Barbara, Calif., Clio Press, 1971).
Has chapter on United Nations publications.

Statistical Information

The research worker in any social subject inevitably amasses a collection of statistical data for himself and makes appropriate use of it. Apart from this material, however, there is frequent need for statistical information of the type assiduously collected by many official organisations, ranging from international bodies, through national governments and their ministries and bureaux, to the data compiled by voluntary organisations of many kinds. Statistics collection is indeed a major governmental occupation. There is even in Britain, a Central Statistical Office which, though important, handles only a proportion of the statistics compiled, utilised and published by the government. There exist certain publications which act as guides to particular kinds of statistics, sometimes describing the methods by which they are collected and giving valuable guidance on where, in published series, they are to be found. Examples of these include:

(i) *Sources of Statistics*, by Joan M. Harvey (2nd ed., London, Clive Bingley, 1971).
Includes chapters on social problems, education, population and health statistics.

(ii) *List of Principal Statistical Series and Publications.* Central Statistical Office (3 vols., London, H.M.S.O., 1972).

No. 20 of Studies in Official Statistics series. *Statistical News* (see v below) provides updating service.
(iii) *Recommended Basic Statistical Sources* (London, Library Association, 1969).
(iv) *Guides to Official Sources.* Interdepartmental Committee on Social and Economic Research (London, H.M.S.O.).
Guides in this series include:
(a) Labour statistics (rev. ed. 1958).
(b) Social security statistics (1961).

Details of new official statistical publications in Britain may be found in a periodical issued by the Central Statistical Office.

(v) *Statistical News: Developments in British Official Statistics* (London, H.M.S.O., 1968– . Quarterly).

Equivalent guides for United States statistical services include:

(vi) *Statistics Sources,* by P. Wasserman (3rd ed., Detroit, Mich., Gale, 1971).

Amongst the numerous statistical series available, the following U.K. sources may be noted:

(vii) *Monthly Digest of Statistics* (London, H.M.S.O., 1946–).
This forms the basis for a yearly collection:
(viii) *Annual Abstract of Statistics* (London, H.M.S.O., Vol. 84, 1948–). This was previously entitled: *Statistical Abstract for the United Kingdom,* Vols. 1–83, 1854–1940.
(ix) *Social Trends* (London, H.M.S.O., 1970–).
This is a new annual publication of the Central Statistical Office and covers population, employment, leisure, social services, education, housing; with selected international comparisons.
(x) *Scottish Social Work Statistics* (Edinburgh, H.M.S.O., 1971–). Produced by the Social Work Service Group of the Scottish Education Department.
(xi) *Welfare Service Statistics* (London, Institute of Municipal Treasurers and Accountants and Society of County Treasurers, Annual).

(xii) *Britain in Figures,* by A. F. Sillitoe (2nd ed., Harmondsworth, Penguin, 1973). Presents selected contemporary social statistics in readily assimilable graph, diagram or chart form.

(xiii) *Social Security Statistics.* Department of Health and Social Security (London, H.M.S.O., Annual).
First published in 1973, provides statistical data to accompany department's annual report.

(xiv) *Health and Personal Social Services Statistics.* Department of Health and Social Security (London, H.M.S.O., 1972–).
Continued from *Digest of Health Statistics* (1969–72).

Statistics for regions of Britain are also available annually in: *Abstract of Regional Statistics* (Central Statistical Office); *Digest of Welsh Statistics* (Welsh Office); *Scottish Abstracts of Statistics* (Scottish Office); *Digest of Statistics, Northern Ireland.*

Similar publications may be located for other countries in guides such as that by Wasserman (vi, above). International coverage is provided by several United Nations series:

(xv) *Statistical Yearbook* (New York, U.N., Vol. 1, 1948–).
Brought up to date by:

(xvi) *Monthly Bulletin of Statistics.*

(xvii) *Report on the World Social Situation* (New York, U.N., Bureau of Social Affairs, 1958–).

(xviii) *Compendium of Social Statistics* (New York, U.N., 1963–).

(xix) *Basic Facts and Figures* (Paris, Unesco, 1958–).

Demographic and related statistics are to be found in the publications of the Census Offices; for example, the British Office of Population Censuses and Surveys (previously the General Register Office) and the United States Census Office. The United Nations Statistical Office produces:

(xx) *Demographic Yearbook* (New York, U.N., 1948–).
Emphasises one particular aspect each year.

Finally, guidance on handling statistics is offered by:

(xxi) *Use of Official Statistics in Sociology,* by B. Hindess (London, Macmillan, 1973).

Directories

There is frequently a need to establish which organisations or individuals are important in some particular activity or are engaged in some particular research; directories and yearbooks will provide name and address information of this kind. Some appropriate ones are:

(i)   *Social Services Year Book* (London, Councils and Education Press, 1973/4). ("The intention is that it should contain pretty well every item of directory material concerning the social services in the U.K. that anyone could reasonably want to look for". Foreword.)

(ii) *Social Services in Britain.* Issued by the Central Office of Information (new ed., London, H.M.S.O., 1966).

(iii) *Public Social Services* (13th ed., National Council of Social Service, 1973). With supplements.

(iv) *Guide to the Social Services* (London, Family Welfare Association, Annual).

(v)   *Voluntary Social Services* (new ed., London, National Council of Social Service, 1973).

(vi) *Consumer's Guide to the British Social Services*, by P. Willmott (Harmondsworth, Penguin Books, 1967).

(vii) *Welfare Services Manual* (London, British Red Cross, 1963).

(viii) *Charities Digest* (London, Family Welfare Association and Butterworths, Annual). Classified arrangement with alphabetical index.

(ix) *Directory of Grant-making Trusts* (London, National Council of Social Services, 1968).

(x)   *Directory of Child Guidance and School Psychological Services in England and Wales* (London, National Association for Mental Health, 1970).

(xi) *Yearbook of the Youth Service in England and Wales* (London, Youth Service Information Centre, 1970/71).

(xii) *Probation and After-care Directory* (London, H.M.S.O., Annual).

(xiii) *Directory of Prison After-care Projects* (2nd ed., London, National Association of Discharged Prisoners' Aid Societies, 1966).

(xiv)   *NACRO Manual and Directory* (London, National Association for the Care and Resettlement of Offenders, 1973).

(xv)   *British Health Centres Directory* (London, King Edward's Hospital Fund for London, 1973).

Periodical Literature

The periodical is at present the most important medium of dissemination of new knowledge. It has existed in more or less the form we know it for about three hundred years, dating back to the days of the *Philosophical Transactions* of the Royal Society in Britain and the *Journal des Scavans* in France. Recent research, development and methodology are reported in journals and this is only later distilled and rehashed in books. It can be said that most of the material in periodicals never appears in books at all. Other uses of journals as organs of professional societies and as providers of current information of general interest to their readers can be for the moment disregarded here, because it is their importance as a repository of new knowledge which may be located by the research worker which is of immediate concern.

The number of learned journals is now extremely great and represents an amount of literature which no one, however narrow his speciality, can find time adequately to read and digest. Whilst the specialist knows well which are the most important journals from his own point of view, other seekers of information on a particular topic are not necessarily so fortunately placed and require a guide through a pretty large field. The searcher may first require to know the names of journals covering the social sciences and here general guides as well as more specialised ones can be of assistance. Amongst these may be included:

(i)   *Ulrich's International Periodicals Directory* (15th ed., New York, Bowker, 1973/4). Gives full details of 55,000 periodicals.

(ii)   *Guide to Current British Journals*, by David Woodworth (2nd ed., London, Library Association, 1973). This has a more limited coverage than (i) and the emphasis is obvious from the title. The number of periodicals briefly described and categorised by subjects is well below 4000 as compared with Ulrich's 50,000. Two volumes—volume 2 is a directory of publishers.

There are certain lists of periodicals which are limited by subject. These may be identified by their subject in works such as:

(iii) *Guides to Scientific Periodicals*, by Maureen Fowler (London, Library Association, 1966).

Important lists include:

(iv) *World List of Social Science Periodicals* (3rd ed., Paris, Unesco, 1966). At the time of this edition there were known to be more than 1300 social science periodicals currently published.

There is a similar list of periodicals in a related field:

(v) *Educational Periodicals.* International Directories of Education Service (2nd ed., Paris, Unesco, 1963).

Few libraries can hope to subscribe to more than a fraction of the relevant journals, and co-operation between them is necessary to discover what is to be found in each. This is achieved by union catalogues, of which excellent examples are:

(vi) *British Union Catalogue of Periodicals* (London, Butterworths, 1956–60 to date). This gives the location of over 150,000 periodicals.

(vii) *World List of Scientific Periodicals* (3 vols., 4th ed., London, Butterworths, 1963–5). This covers more than 60,000 titles published during the years 1900–60, with locations for each. Now continued by the *British Union Catalogue* (see vi).

(viii) *Union List of Serials in the Libraries of the United States and Canada* (5 vols, 3rd ed., New York, Wilson, 1965). Titles and locations of more than 150,000 periodicals.

Many libraries issue their own list of holdings, and an example of this is:

(ix) *Current Periodicals in the National Lending Library for Science and Technology* (Boston Spa, National Lending Library, 1971).

Major libraries occasionally provide a list as part of their printed catalogue as in the case of the London School of Economics (Volume IV of *London Bibliography of the Social Sciences*) and the British Museum (*General Catalogue*, volume covering "Periodical Publications").

Abstracts and Indexes

Two factors make it imperative for a research worker to be aware of and familiar with abstracts and indexing journals; these are: the existence of an extremely large number of periodicals in which relevant work might be reported; and the "scatter" whereby the majority of papers for which a particular worker may have need at any time is to be found in journals in which he would not normally look. The abstracting and indexing services scan issues of periodicals in their own subject, and for all relevant articles—in the case of abstracts—produce a summary which may be brief and only indicative, or larger and thereby more informative. The indexing services merely list author, title and bibliographical details of the periodical or other publication in which the article appeared. Entries are normally arranged by subject, either alphabetically or by some systematic form of grouping. They thus facilitate subject search in the periodical literature and provide access to information which is fairly recent. The time-lag in the preparation of the abstracts and in publication of the journal in which they are contained can be considerable and users should bear this in mind if seeking up-to-the-minute information. This need in social science subjects may not be great.

The first requirement for successful use of these facilities is awareness of the appropriate abstract or indexing journals—and there is a considerable amount of overlap and duplication, coupled with gaps in effective coverage. Guides to the services will suggest the best journals or bibliographies to consult. Such guides are:

(i) *Abstracting Services*. Issued by the International Federation for Documentation (The Hague, F.I.D., 1963).

(ii) *Index Bibliographicus*, Vol. 1, *Humanities and Social Science* (4th ed., F.I.D., 1964, The Hague).

Each gives details of many hundreds of useful services for a wide range of subjects. For convenience some of the most important are listed below:

GENERAL

   (iii) *British Humanities Index* (London, Library Association, 1964–). Preceded by *Subject Index to Periodicals*, 1916–63.
   (iv) *Social Sciences and Humanities Index* (New York, Wilson, 1965–). Preceded by *International Index*, 1916–64.
    (v) *Readers' Guide to Periodical Literature* (New York, Wilson, 1905–).
   (vi) *Public Affairs Information Service. Bulletin* (New York, P.A.I.S., 1915–).
  (vii) *Monthly List of Selected Articles* (Geneva, United Nations Library, 1929–).
 (viii) *Internationale Bibliographie der Zeitschriften Literatur* (Osnabrück, Dietrich Verlag). (Section A covers German and Section B covers non-German periodical literature in all fields of knowledge.)

SOCIOLOGY

   (ix) *Sociological Abstracts* (New York, American Sociological Association, 1953–).
    (x) *Bulletin Signalétique*, Section 21, *Sociologie. Sciences des Langage*; Section 19, *Philosophie. Sciences Humaines* (Paris, C.N.R.S., 1961–).
   (xi) *International Bibliography of the Social Sciences. Sociology* (London, Tavistock, 1960). (An annual index with excellent coverage and indexing.)
  (xii) *ABS Guide to Recent Publications in the Social and Behavioral Sciences* (American Behavioral Scientist, 1965). With annual supplements.

SOCIAL WORK

 (xiii) *Abstracts for Social Workers* (New York, National Association of Social Workers, 1965–).

LAW AND CRIMINOLOGY

(xiv) *Crime and Delinquency Abstracts* (National Clearing House for Mental Health Information, U.S.D.H.E.W., 1963–72). Previously *International Bibliography on Crime and Delinquency*, 1963–5.

(xv) *Abstracts on Criminology and Penology* (Deventer, The Netherlands, Kluwer, 1961–). Previously *Excerpta Criminology*, 1961–8.

(xvi) *Index to Legal Periodicals* (New York, Wilson, 1926–).

EDUCATION

(xvii) *Education Index* (New York, Wilson, 1929–).

(xviii) *British Education Index* (London, Library Association, 1954–).

(xix) *Sociology of Education Abstracts* (London, Information for Education Ltd., 1965–).

(xx) *Current Index to Journals in Education* (New York, Macmillan, 1969–). Published for the U.S. Educational Resources Information Center.

PSYCHOLOGY

(xxi) *Psychological Abstracts* (Washington, American Psychological Association, 1927–).

(xxii) *Child Development Abstracts and Bibliography* (Chicago, University of Chicago Press, 1927–). Published for the Society for Research in Child Development.

(xxiii) *Bulletin Signalétique.* Section 20, *Psychologie, Pédegogie* (Paris, C.N.R.S., 1961–).

(xxiv) *Index Medicus* (Washington, National Library of Medicine and U.S.D.H.E.W., 1960–). Annual form: *Cumulated Index Medicus*. Published with various titles since 1879.

Similar publications cover other social science areas, notably politics, economics, social anthropology.

An excellent current awareness service alerting readers to new papers in relevant periodicals is available:

(xxv)   *Current Contents: Social and Behavioral Sciences* (Philadelphia, Institute for Scientific Information, 1969–　).

A new reference tool for the social sciences periodical literature is now available:

(xxvi)   *Social Sciences Citation Index* (Philadelphia, Institute for Scientific Information, 1973–　). Enables identification of all papers citing a known work. Subject approach also possible.

Literature Searching

Sufficient indication has been given of the categories of material available for exploitation in a good library and it seems appropriate to consider now the sequence of steps which might be taken to produce a comprehensive list of references to published work in a given topic. Treatment will be brief and actual works will not be cited. Use will be made of the terminology already employed and elucidated.

At the outset the researcher must define clearly and precisely the subject of his search. This should be set down in words and some initial thought given to all the associated terms which will be the words under which the subject indexes will be searched. Synonyms, popular terms and transatlantic variations must be noted.

The search will proceed from the known to the unknown; from the general to the specific. General and special dictionaries and encyclopaedias may be an apt starting point. From the latter, relevant standard books in the subject might be found. Library catalogues, including that in his own library, should be consulted by the researcher and appropriate books noted. As the classification systems in most libraries result in general subjects appearing—in the classified catalogues and on the shelves—ahead of the branches and subdivisions of the subject, it is well to remember that certain information may be contained in a more general book.

The existence of a bibliography on the subject under consideration could next be determined by consulting a bibliography of bibliographies. The library catalogue could also reveal a bibliography and likewise indicate if there were any review series in which a state-of-the-art survey might be expected.

All books—including those not in stock in the researcher's own library—could be identified and details obtained from the volumes of national or trade bibliographies. Geographical and language limitations would be set by the research worker himself.

For official publications of governments and international bodies the appropriate catalogues should then be scanned. These might also include reports commissioned by government agencies.

Information regarding recent theses or current research should be obtained from indexes of such activity.

Having exhausted the non-periodical literature, the next step would be to survey the output in journals via the abstracts and indexing services. This would have to be done painstakingly and comprehensively. The obvious abstracting services would be checked first and the other, less-known or unknown ones would be identified by a guide to them, and then these journals too would be systematically checked.

The breadth and depth of the searching should be determined by the searcher before he begins, so that he knows, for example, whether to include publications in foreign languages, and which; whether to go back more than a few years and, if so, how far; whether to range widely over the subject or look for one very specific topic and no other. The searcher should not be afraid to alter the pattern of his search or set different limits as he goes along, because he can quickly form an opinion as the search proceeds about the way the topic has been written up.

Where necessary, the search must be brought right up to date by perusal of latest copies of those journals which the check of the abstracts has revealed to be most fruitful. These later journals and the articles in them may well lead to further references which had somehow escaped the main search process.

By now the important early—or original—papers and books, the significant new ones and any large-scale reviews of work will probably have come to light and the next step—the reading process—can begin. Some evaluation of the remaining titles on the list can be done and efforts got under way to obtain the items directly from the researcher's own library or by the inter-library loan system.

CHAPTER 5

The Use of Data Analysis and the Principles
of Probability Theory

IN a previous chapter the research process was examined in some detail to enable us to examine the steps separately, but also to show that each process was inter-dependent and the steps necessarily linked. Although the process may be conceived of as being a complete step in itself, it is only the means to a more important end; the process is to ensure that answers can be provided which will enable the researcher to relate them to the perceived problem to provide a solution or a better understanding of the observed difficulty.

A necessary step between the collection of data and drawing meaningful inferences from them is that of statistical analysis. We have already indicated that this is a step which should be planned for the research design so that the researcher will know precisely how he intends to make this link, and in the chapters which follow a variety of statistical techniques are described in detail in order to achieve this end. However, underlying all of these techniques are the principles of *probability theory* and it is necessary for the reader to understand these principles so that he can appreciate and accept the validity of the techniques which are subsequently described.

A major reason for conducting research is to enable us to make predictions about what *will* be, given that the elements under study are held constant. If our Example 1 (page 26) which hypothesised that *there will be no difference in the effectiveness of treatment between a group of professionally trained social workers and a group of untrained social workers* yielded data which disproved the hypothesis, we could predict with some accuracy that effectiveness would always be related to training if all else remained constant (e.g. the clients, the workers, the training, etc.). Given that this was true we could then feel reasonably confident in recommending that all social workers should be trained. If our recommendations were accepted we might also reasonably predict that the help given to clients would be more effective.

Principles of Probability

Once the results of a study have been obtained by following the research process, we have reached a stage where new problems emerge; our crude results themselves have to be subjected to other processes in order to determine their usefulness. In other words we have to decide whether the picture presented by these results is sufficiently meaningful for inferences to be drawn on which further action can be taken or whether the results could be simply the result of chance. If the latter is operative, then it would be extremely unwise to proceed to further action (research, policy decisions, etc.) since our observations may not be valid. Using our Example 2 hypothesis (page 29), if it was found that the number of cases which came to the agency on any specific day exceeded the number coming on other days we might be tempted into acting on this information by having more social workers in the agency on that day, but flaws are inherent in making such a decision. For example, the steps involved in the research process may not have been applied with sufficient rigor and this could result in such errors as:

(a) *Sample bias*—A bus strike on particular days on consecutive weeks could affect the pattern of clients visiting the agency.
(b) Some social workers in the agency may, for a variety of reasons, have omitted to record details of all the clients they saw during the period under study.
(c) The timing of the study could have spanned a holiday period.
(d) Visits could have been recorded under the wrong day.

Whilst errors of this nature could have been circumvented by a more rigorous approach during the research process, the results of the study could be explained by finding, in retrospect, that events such as those listed had occurred. Clearly, how one used the findings would be influenced by the knowledge that observable occurrences could explain a difference in the numbers of clients who visited the agency on any particular day of the week.

If, however, no such explanations were apparent, this could mean that whilst they were *not apparent*, nevertheless they existed. It could be postulated that there was no particular reason for variations in the numbers of clients who called on particular days of the week—that it was pure "chance" that one day was chosen rather than another. Therefore, it is necessary to find ways of determining whether or not our findings are chance ones or whether more time and energy need to be expended in order to explain the findings. If the variations were not due to chance alone then no action can be taken on the findings until we have a fairly good reason to explain why they have occurred or, in the absence of this, near certain knowledge that the pattern was likely to be repeated in the future. Even without the ability to observe "cause and effect", if the findings could not be explained by chance and if we studied the phenomenon observed accurately and over a sufficiently long period of time and still found the same inexplicable findings, some administrative action would be warranted. For example, we could reorganise staff activities so that more staff could be available in the agency on the days when most clients called and conduct their home visits on the days when fewest called. However, if the results of the study could be explained as being purely "chance" findings, then major staff redeployment would clearly be unwise. It therefore becomes imperative that we know how to process our findings in order to eliminate the possibility of their being the results of chance or to be able to accept them because "chance" was an unlikely explanation.

Nothing pertaining to the future can be known with absolute certainty and human activity is based largely upon rational assumptions. If there is no apparent logical reason why half of the population should be absent from work or school with illness tomorrow or next week, we make the assumption that this would be a most unlikely event. Such an assumption is based on our previous knowledge and experience. There is no proof that the sun will rise tomorrow, but again the chances that it will not are so small as to be unworthy of consideration. In crossing the street we know that the chances of being knocked down by a motor car are only one in many thousands. If we believed that the chances were one in ten, or one in two, then we might well stop at home! With much of human endeavour, we do not accurately estimate the probabilities of a particular event occurring but make a common sense assumption. We may all think that we will live to be about 70 years old, but assurance companies need to calculate the probability much more accurately than this. The fact that reputable companies rarely go bankrupt is perhaps indicative of the fact that calculations based on probability theory are valid for estimating the likelihood of a particular event occurring in the future.

Although probability theory enables us to estimate the likelihood of a particular event occurring, it can make no ultimate contribution to determining whether or not a particular course of action *should* be followed. A medical specialist may say that an operation has a 90% chance of success, but what he generally means is that nine out of ten people of similar age, physical condition, attitude towards illness and similarity of complaint have, to his knowledge, benefited by this particular operation. The doctor cannot tell which patient out of ten will be the unfortunate one. Whether or not a nine out of ten chance of the probability of success is good enough must be decided by the patient. Some will take a one in a hundred chance; others look for near certainty.

The social scientist and the social worker are particularly interested in probabilities concerning certain future events. For example, we have indicated by our hypothesis 2 (page 29) that for good staff management and the best interests of clients it would be desirable to predict with some certainty which days of the week would make most demands on the staff. Although there is much value in the practical implications of questions which involve probability principles, they themselves can probably be more easily grasped not with social science examples but from examples based on games of chance from which probability theory was first developed. However, before embarking on a full explanation of probability theory the reader should be given a definition of probability.

> *The probability of an event or a combination of events is dependent on the ratio of the number of ways in which the event or events can occur to the total number of ways the event or events can occur.*

For example, if a single coin is tossed, the total number of ways that the coin can land is two, either "heads" or "tails". We cannot predict with any certainty which face of the coin will land uppermost, but we can say that the probability of it being either head or tails will be equal. In other words there are two possibilities for the outcome which give a ratio for each event being equal to 0.5.

If, on tossing the coin once, a "head" lands uppermost, what is the probability of getting a "head" on the second or subsequent throws? Despite intuitive feelings that the probability should be less, it will remain exactly the same at a one in two chance, since each toss is a separate event.

Coin tossing as a game of chance usually involves the tossing of *two* coins and we will examine such a game where money is being wagered on the result. The tosser is expected to produce either two heads or two tails from a couple of pennies and people will wager with one another on the outcome of either of these two possibilities. The third possibility, the result being a head and a tail does not count in the wager and the tosser repeats his action until two heads or two tails are obtained.

We said the probability of getting either of two heads or two tails was two to one because the probability of an event occurring is the ratio of the number of ways in which a particular event can occur to the total number of possible outcomes. In tossing two coins on one occasion, the total possible outcomes are:

Two heads
One head and one tail
One tail and one head
Two tails

By chance a "head, head" outcome would occur once in four throws, a "tail, tail" would also occur once in four throws, while "one of each" would happen twice in four throws. From this we can see that probability (denoted by p) is multiplicative. For any single coin that we toss the odds against obtaining a head or a tail are two to one, i.e. $p = 0.5$. When we toss two coins together the odds against a "head, head" or "tail, tail" outcome are two to one *times* two to one, that is $(\frac{1}{2} \times \frac{1}{2}) = \frac{1}{4}$, and $p = 0.25$. The odds against "one of each" are two to one since "head, tail" and "tail, head" give the same answer:

$$(\tfrac{1}{2} \times \tfrac{1}{2}) + (\tfrac{1}{2} \times \tfrac{1}{2}) = \tfrac{1}{4} + \tfrac{1}{4} = \tfrac{1}{2}, p = 0.5.$$

In general terms the value of p is obtained by dividing the desired outcome by the total number of possible outcomes. In tossing two coins there are four possible outcomes and for each coin a head or a tail has an equal chance of occurring. If one of our coins were double-headed then probabilities of the various permutations would change. Tossing our normal coin four times would yield two heads and two tails while for our biased coin the result would always be heads. Thus, the probability of a "head, head" outcome would be $(\frac{1}{2} \times 1) = \frac{1}{2}$ or $p = 0.5$, that of a "tail, tail" outcome would be $(\frac{1}{2} \times 0) = 0$, that of "one of each" would be $(\frac{1}{2} \times 1) + (\frac{1}{2} \times 0) = \frac{1}{2}$ or $p = 0.5$. The probability of an occurrence can take any value from 0 to 1; in tossing our double-headed penny there is no chance of obtaining a tail and its p is equal to 0. For the same coin the probability of obtaining a head is 1. For any instance the probabilities of all alternative outcomes add to unity.

Let us go beyond the once only situation and see what the probability of getting say "head, head" on two consecutive throws of the coins. Throwing two unbiased coins on consecutive tosses is exactly like throwing four coins at the same time. The chances of getting "head, head, head, head" are $(\frac{1}{2} \times \frac{1}{2} \times \frac{1}{2} \times \frac{1}{2}) = \frac{1}{16}$, $p = 0.062$. Each toss of two coins is an independent event with four possible outcomes. The probability of any particular outcome occurring twice in succession is obtained by multiplying its probability of occurrence on the first occasion by its probability of occurrence on the second. If we consider dice-throwing we know that for a single die there are six possible outcomes for any one throw, while for two dice there are 6×6 possible outcomes in each throw.

The tossing of a number of coins on a number of occasions leads to a most important theoretical concept which has value for much statistical work, that of the *binomial distribution*. This is a theoretical frequency distribution of the number of occasions that a particular outcome will be obtained in repeated trials of independent events, all of constant probability.

The following are the characteristics of the binomial distribution:

1. Every event (or trial) has two possible outcomes—no more, no less. A trial with more than two possible outcomes can contribute

to a binomial distribution, providing that all the outcomes except two are ignored or otherwise eliminated.

2. Each particular outcome must have a constant probability for all trials. The two outcomes need not have the same probability but each must be unchanging.

3. Each outcome must be completely independent of all other outcomes. Even although two pennies may have landed "both heads" on ninety-nine consecutive occasions and, humanly, it seems most unlikely that it can happen for the hundredth time, nonetheless the probability of a further two heads is still 0.25. This independence of each separate trial is necessary for the binomial distribution.

4. There must be a number of events so that each does not disproportionately affect a total outcome.

If we tossed three coins together, the following would be the possible alternatives:

$$
\begin{array}{c}
\text{HHH} \\
\text{HHT} \\
\text{HTH} \\
\text{HTT} \\
\text{THH} \\
\text{THT} \\
\text{TTH} \\
\text{TTT}
\end{array}
$$

Consequently, the chances of getting:

no heads would be one chance in eight or 0.125
one head would be three chances in eight or 0.375.

The chances of getting two heads also would be three chances in eight or 0.375.

The relative expected frequency for any one outcome (e.g. one head or one tail) can be calculated for the tossing of ten coins and these would be:

TABLE 5.1.

Number of 'heads'	Percentage of all coins	Expected relative frequency
0	0	0.001
1	10	0.010
2	20	0.045
3	30	0.117
4	40	0.205
5	50	0.246
6	60	0.205
7	70	0.117
8	80	0.045
9	90	0.010
10	100	0.001
Total		1.000

As the number of trials are increased, so is the distribution concentrated around the central value, in this case 5, and each additional outcome makes a decreasingly significant contribution to the total outcome. If a very large number of trials are made, the result is a continuous frequency distribution. Such a smoothed binomial curve is known as a normal distribution. Normal distributions have a number of mathematical properties which are very useful to statisticians. Some of these are discussed in the next chapter.

Use of the normal distribution curve enables us to calculate probability values for various occurrences. For example, let us consider one possibility following from our Example 1 hypothesis (see page 26). We might observe that out of the group of professionally trained social workers, one worker claimed successful treatment with 62 of his 100 clients while the average for all trained social workers under study was 70 per 100 clients. Using a number of the statistical procedures to be dealt with in Chapter 6 it was found that the probability of an individual social worker differing by 8 from the group average was 0.228. We would conclude that about two workers in every ten in this study would show such a discrepancy in their reported success.

There is no hard and fast rule concerning the probability levels which can be accepted as being so unlikely to have occurred by chance that some other explanation must be sought. The most commonly accepted *statistically significant* level is that where the probability of some occurrence being due to chance is less than five occurrences in every hundred occasions, expressed as $p < 0.05$.

It is quite possible to set up other criteria for *statistical significance*; we could accept a probability of one in ten or one in ten thousand as being appropriate. If our criteria for statistical significance are not sufficiently stringent, then we might reject the null hypothesis in our experiment when in fact it is true. On the other hand, if our criterion is too demanding, then we may accept the null hypothesis when it is in fact false. These errors are inversely related so that the more we guard against the one the more we expose ourselves to the other. In short, we could caution the reader against being too adamant about any inferences he draws from statistical analysis, since he can never be absolutely certain that his findings are error free.

CHAPTER 6

Simple Descriptive Statistics

ONCE we have decided what variables we are interested in and what kinds of scale we can legitimately use to measure different "amounts" of each variable, we must then decide how we shall *tabulate* the scores on our variables, that is to say how we shall arrange the scores in an orderly manner.

Let us look at tabulation using the following example which could have been derived from the study involved in the testing of hypothesis (page 29). The ages of all new clients attending a social work agency over a 2-week period were recorded. Thirty new clients were seen and their ages appear in Table 6.1.

TABLE 6.1

Client	Age	Client	Age	Client	Age
1	25	11	42	21	29
2	24	12	52	22	31
3	21	13	61	23	37
4	21	14	54	24	28
5	31	15	31	25	22
6	26	16	32	26	52
7	19	17	20	27	23
8	25	18	26	28	44
9	24	19	28	29	58
10	26	20	25	30	40

It is very difficult to extract any meaningful information about the ages of clients from this table. The simplest form of tabulation in this case would be to arrange the data so that the ages would be ranked in sequence from the highest, client 13 (61 years), to the lowest, client 7 (19 years). This method lets us see that three clients are aged 25 years, two are aged 21 years and so on. Such a tabulation gives a *frequency distribution* of ages for our sample of clients. It is quite laborious to carry out this kind of frequency distribution and as the number of cases increases it ceases to be a practical proposition. When arranging the frequency distribution of a large number of scores we first group the possible scores into *class intervals*—symbolised as i.

Consider Table 6.2. We have formed class intervals for age so that we have groups covering 5-year intervals. Thus, the lowest interval group includes ages 15, 16, 17, 18 and 19. Class intervals must be chosen with care so that while they are large enough, say up to twenty, to facilitate tabulation by grouping ages together they must be small enough, say one to five, to be used in further statistical calculations. For any variable the wider the class interval, the fewer the categories or groups. For most social data it will be best to use between six and fifteen categories, all of which will, of course, be the same size.

TABLE 6.2

Age group	Frequency
60–64	1
55–59	1
50–54	3
45–49	0
40–44	3
35–39	1
30–34	4
25–29	9
20–24	7
15–19	1
Class interval = 5	No. of cases (N) = 30

From Table 6.2 we can see that the age group with most clients is the 25–29 years group closely followed by the 20–24 years group. It is common practice to present such frequency distributions graphically in the form of histograms as shown in Fig. 6.1.

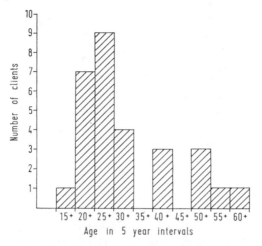

FIG. 6.1. Histogram of data from Table 6.2.

Histograms can be used to present qualitative as well as quantitative data. Figure 6.1 shows the number of clients in each age group. The method can just as easily show the number of clients who are grouped according to social class, marital status or the like. It is important to remember in all graphical representations of this kind that the axes of the graphs are clearly labelled and carry a clear indication of the scale being used.

The Misuse of Graphical Representations of Data

Graphical representations of data have "eye appeal". The main salients are at once apparent to the eye of the consumer who is saved the tedium of scanning columns of figures. This instant, intuitive appeal often leads to graphs being used to misrepresent data. There are three main forms of misrepresentation: (1) the graph is not properly labelled, (2) the scales used are out of balance, (3) the graph contains only selected portions of the available data. Examples of these abuses are shown in Figs. 6.2–6.4. It is easy to see that with a combination of these abuses statistics really can lie!

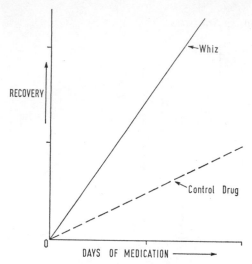

FIG. 6.2. A common misuse: what do the labels tell you?
CAPTION: "Whiz gets your patients better faster".

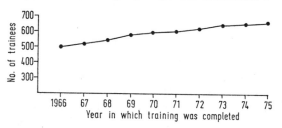

CAPTION A. "There has been no increase in the number of social worker trainees".

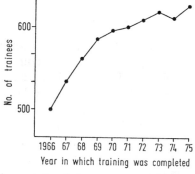

CAPTION B. "The past decade has seen a vast increase in the number of social worker trainees."

FIG. 6.3. The data is the same. See what changing the scale does!

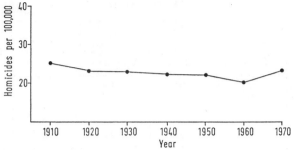

CAPTION A. "Northland's homicide rate is below the prewar level."

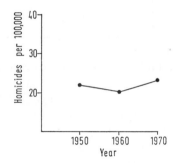

CAPTION B. "Northland's homicide rate has risen in the past decade."

FIG. 6.4. The data is the same—just be selective!

Tabulating More than One Variable

Table 6.2 is an example of an *univariate* table of distribution, dealing, as it does, with only one variable. *Bivariate* tables deal with the distributions of two variables simultaneously. For example, using our hypothesis 2 (page 29) we might want to examine the ages of our clients in relation to their marital state and this is shown in Table 6.3. In this presentation the class interval has been extended from five to ten.

On the vertical and horizontal margins of the table we have the frequency distributions of the variables considered separately while in the body of the table we have the frequencies of the combined characteristics

TABLE 6.3. MARITAL STATE OF CLIENTS

Age group	Single	Married	Widowed	Separated or divorced	Frequency distribution for age
55–64	1	0	1	0	2
45–54	0	0	1	2	3
35–44	1	2	0	1	4
25–34	5	8	0	0	13
15–24	5	3	0	0	8
Frequency distribution for marital state	12	13	2	3	No. of clients $(N) = 30$

measured. From a table such as this we can say that eight of the thirty clients are in the 15–24 age group, that thirteen of the thirty are married, that five clients are single and aged 25–34 years and so on.

Bivariate tables of this kind lead to questions about differences in the frequencies being related, for instance "Are differences in marital state related to age?" Such questions can be answered by using statistical tests which will be described later.

Measures of Central Tendency

We have shown how some information about the ages of the thirty clients listed in Table 6.1 can be displayed by the use of frequency distributions and graphs, but how should we answer the question "What is the average age of these clients?" In everyday language we use the term "average" in two main ways; we use it to denote the most typical or the most frequent value on some variable, e.g. "the average family has two children", or we use it to denote a value which will be most representative of all the values obtained for a group, e.g. "the average basic wage of clients was". In statistical terms the former "average" is called the *mode* and the latter the *mean*.

The mode is the value in a distribution which occurs more frequently than another other value. With nominal data only the mode can be truly representative of the group. If in a social work agency, for example, we have:

six delinquent clients
four unmarried mothers
two child neglect cases and
twenty-four matrimonial cases

then it would be reasonable to say that the matrimonial case was our modal client. We may wish to add that they comprised two-thirds of our total clientele and that the remaining third was made up of three different categories. If the matrimonial cases comprised less than 50% of the total, then it would be most necessary to add this additional information. Where two values share the highest position within a distribution, we would call this a *bimodal* distribution.

The mode is the best indicator of "averageness" or *central tendency* when the variable being studied has what is called a *skewed distribution*, that is, when most values fall at one end of a distribution but there is a sprinkling of values falling at the other end. The number of children in a family is a good example of a skewed distribution. The great majority of families will have one, two or three children, but in a large sample of cases there will be families of nine, ten or more children. So when in using "average" we mean the most common value in a distribution then we seek the *mode*.

The most common measure of central tendency is the *mean*, the most representative value of the distribution. The mean is calculated by adding up all the observed values and dividing by the number of cases observed. To find the mean age of the clients in Table 6.1 we would add up all the ages and divide by thirty, the number of clients. In general terms this is expressed as

$$\text{Mean} = \frac{\Sigma X}{N},$$

Where the Greek letter "capital sigma" (Σ) means "the sum of", X stands for any value of a variable and N represents the number of values observed. The mean is usually denoted by the symbol $\bar{x}$ (called x—bar).

Where data have been formed into a frequency distribution *without class intervals* the mean is calculated using the formula $\bar{x}$ (mean) $= \dfrac{\Sigma fX}{\Sigma f}$, where the top line reads "the sum of each value multiplied by its frequency of occurrence" and the bottom line reads "the sum of all frequencies".

Where we have a frequency distribution with class intervals we can use the above formula provided we assume that the mid point of each class interval takes the value "X". Thus, in Table 6.2 the mid-points of the class intervals which are 62, 57, 52, etc., would be multiplied by their respective frequencies, summed, and divided by the total frequency. This procedure rapidly leads to the calculation of very large sums and it is customary to use the method set out in Table 6.4.

TABLE 6.4

Age group	frequency (f)	deviation from assumed mean (d)	fd	fd^2
60–64	1	+6	6	36
55–59	1	+5	5	25
50–54	3	+4	12	48
45–49	0	+3	0	0
40–44	3	+2	6	12
35–39	1	+1	1	1
30–34	4	0	0	0
25–29	9	−1	−9	9
20–24	7	−2	−14	28
15–19	1	−3	−3	9
Class interval (i) = 5	$\Sigma f = 30$		$\Sigma fd = 4$	$\Sigma fd^2 = 168$

The mean is calculated thus: $\bar{x} = A = \dfrac{i\Sigma fd}{\Sigma f}$

where A is an assumed mean, the mid-point of one of the class intervals from the range, i is the size of the class intervals and fd is the sum of the products of the entries in columns f and d. In this case we have, $\bar{x} = 32$

$$+ \frac{5 \times 4}{30} = 32.666.$$

This value can be compared with that obtained from Table 6.1 when $\bar{x} = 32.566$. The discrepancy is due to the fact that when data is presented in class intervals it has to be assumed that the values occurring in each class interval are equally distributed throughout the class. Deviations from this assumption lead to slight discrepancies in results.

The assumed mean procedure can be understood better if we consider the mean as the centre of gravity of a set of scores. In Fig. 6.5 five children, A to E, of identical weight have been placed on a marked plank. Positioned as they are around the point of balance they demonstrate a simple law of physics. The moments of force around the point of balance (point 7 in Fig. 6.5), the sum of each product of mass times

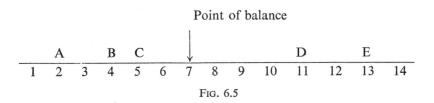

Point of balance

FIG. 6.5

distance, balance exactly. That is, if each child weighed 4 stones their weights multiplied by the distance from the point of balance summed for each side of the plank would balance. Expressed numerically, the following equation results:

Left side of plank	Right side of plank
A = 4 (7 − 2) = 20 B = 4 (7 − 4) = 12 C = 4 (7 − 5) = 8	D = 4 (7 − 11) = −16 E = 4 (7 − 13) = −24
Total = 40	Total = −40

Since in our example the mass of each child is the same, the moments can be read off as distances from the centre of gravity. If we think of the positions of the children on the plank as scores on some variable, then the mean value, the "centre of gravity", is the point where the positive deviations and negative deviations balance exactly. The algebraic sum of deviations about a mean is always zero so that we can express the mean as:

$$\bar{x} = \bar{x} + 0$$

mean score = mean score + sum of moments about the mean.

Applying the physical model of Fig. 6.5 to the data in Table 6.4 we can think of frequency (f) as mass and deviation (d) as distance then the sum of moments about the mean is expressed as Σfd.

When we assume or guess at the mean, then the better our guess is, the smaller Σfd will be; if we guess exactly, then of course $fd = 0$.

So when we use $\bar{x} = A$ (assumed mean) $+ \dfrac{i\Sigma fd}{f}$, the last part of the formula corrects our estimate of the mean. Where Σfd is zero, then $\dfrac{i\Sigma fd}{f}$ is also zero; if Σfd departs from zero, then the assumed mean is increased or made less by the amount needed to balance the deviations.

The third form of average which is commonly used is the *median*. This is the point in the data where half the number of observations fall above the median and half fall below.

In order to calculate the median, it is necessary to order the cases being studied from the lowest to the highest (or vice versa) and isolate the one in the middle of the distribution.

EXAMPLE:

Years of experience of a group of social workers
2   4   7   8   9   10   11   11   15

Median = 9 years experience.

This is obtained by taking the figure in the middle of an ordered distribution; technically where there is an odd number of cases in the distribution, the median is the number which is:

$$\frac{Number\ of\ cases + 1}{2}.$$

Where there is an even number of cases, the median numbers would be the two in the middle of the ordered distribution or:

$$\frac{Number\ of\ cases}{2} \quad \text{and} \quad \frac{Number\ of\ cases + 2}{2}.$$

Usually it is expected that only a single number will be presented and to obtain this we interpolate for the median.

EXAMPLE:

Years of experience of a group of social workers
2   4   7   8   10   12   14   14   15   19

The median numbers would be 10 and 12. For a single figure, however, we would say that the median number of years of experience was 11.

The use of the median is of particular value:

1. When a distribution is badly skewed and the giving of undue weight to the extremes is to be avoided.
2. When some of the extreme values are not accurately shown.
3. When the time factor is important and large numbers are involved.

It follows that it is helpful to know what type of measure of central tendency is being used in any situation. We hear a lot about averages, but are not usually told what type. A person attempting to stress a particular issue may be tempted to pick the one that gives most support to his particular viewpoint.

EXAMPLE: In a particular county most people get a very low wage, some get a little more and a few get a great deal. We have then a positively skewed distribution. In this situation

1. A person trying to get financial help for the county generally would quote the modal wage (the lowest average).
2. A rich man, attempting to show that he was not much better off

than the rest of the county would quote the mean (the highest average and one to which salaries like his own had influenced considerably).

3. A low wage-earner in seeking to get more would quote his own wage in comparison with the mean—stressing the great disparity between himself and the "average" man.

4. A neutral social scientist, seeing the badly skewed distribution might take the median salary as representative of the country's population.

CHAPTER 7

Measures of Dispersion

IN the previous chapter we discussed the value of ordering, presenting and interpreting data which helps us to describe the characteristics of any distribution. But knowing the average point of a distribution, be it mode, mean or median, by itself is not enough. Take the statement "The mean case load of social workers in Britain is fifty-five." This tells us nothing about how many workers have fewer than ten cases or more than seventy. In describing or talking about a distribution we must know something of how the observed scores are dispersed about the mean.

The simplest index of dispersion is called the *range*. Suppose it was stated in a professional journal that when six experienced social workers were asked to rate the degree of social need in a large number of client families the average agreement between pairs of raters was 77%. On first sight this might be regarded as being quite high. But if the report added that the range of agreement was from 23% to 94% you could say that some pairs of social workers showed almost complete agreement while others showed no agreement worth mentioning. The range is a crude index of dispersion which is used to advantage only when a few observations have been made and more elaborate measures would be inappropriate.

Looking back to Fig. 6.5, we can see that the moments about the mean in our centre of gravity model give some indication of dispersion. However, the sum of these moments or "deviations from the mean" is zero. This is rather unhelpful, but if we squared these deviations from the mean the sum of such squares would give a non-zero figure which could then be used as a basis for measuring dispersion. The most

97

commonly used indicator of dispersion is the *standard deviation*, usually denoted S.D., s.d. or σ, which is a kind of average of all deviations about the mean of a sample.

Its basic formula is:

$$\text{s.d. } (\sigma) = \sqrt{\frac{\Sigma x^2}{N}},$$

where Σx^2 is the sum of the square of each score's difference from the mean and N is the total number of cases.

More simply the process is as follows; calculate the deviation score of each case from the mean, square that value, do likewise for all cases in the sample, add all the squared deviations together, divide that sum by the number of cases in the sample and finally calculate the square root of the dividend.

Where we have grouped data and have used the assumed mean method, as in Table 6.4, we can use the following formula:

$$\text{s.d. } = i \sqrt{\frac{\Sigma fd^2 - \left(\frac{\Sigma fd}{\Sigma f}\right)^2}{\Sigma f}}.$$

That is, we take the sum of values in column fd, divide it by the sum of values in column f and then square the result $\left(\frac{\Sigma fd}{\Sigma f}\right)^2$. We then subtract this value from the sum of values in column fd^2, divide the result by the sum of values in column f, find the square root of the dividend and lastly multiply the square root by i (the size of the class interval). Using the figures from Table 6.4 we have the following values:

$$\text{s.d. } = 5 \sqrt{\frac{168 - \left(\frac{4}{30}\right)^2}{30}}$$

which gives a standard deviation (s.d.) of 11.831.

Where the distribution of the sample has certain characteristics which lead us to call it a *normal distribution*, which will be discussed later (see page 100), the mean and the s.d. are the best measures of central tendency and dispersion. One very useful attribute of the s.d. as a measure of dispersion is that within the range of plus or minus one standard deviation above the mean lie about two-thirds of all cases in the sample. The "ages" example in Table 6.4 gives a sample with a mean of 32.666 and a s.d. of 11.831. In round figures we can then say that two-thirds of the sample will be aged between 21 and 44 years.

Related to the standard deviation is another statistic called the *variance* whose formula is:

$$\frac{\Sigma x^2}{N},$$

that is the sum of each deviation score squared divided by the number of cases in the sample. It is the mean squared deviation of the sample. *The standard deviation is the square root of the variance.*

Both variance and the standard deviation provide measures of the magnitude of individual differences present in a sample. The smaller the s.d. the greater the tendency for scores to be grouped closely around the mean.

Raw Scores and Deviation Scores

It can be a tedious business to calculate deviations from a mean, square them, add them and so on. Where there is access to a calculating machine it is simpler to work with raw scores (i.e. the scores actually recorded), using formulae which have been calculated for this purpose.

It is conventional in statistics to denote a raw score or variable by a capital letter (here we use X), the mean by $\bar{x}$ and a deviation score by a lower case letter, in this case x. Thus we have $x = (X - \bar{x})$, that is, any deviation score is a raw score less the mean score for that sample.

Using a calculating machine we calculate N, the number of cases in the sample, ΣX, the sum of all the raw scores in the sample, and lastly ΣX^2, the sum of each raw score squared. Then the mean is calculated as before, $\bar{x} = \dfrac{\Sigma X}{N}$ and the standard deviation is calculated,

$$\text{s.d.} = \sqrt{\frac{N\Sigma X^2 - (\Sigma X)^2}{N}},$$

that is, the sum of squared raw scores is multiplied by the number of cases and from the product is subtracted the square of the sum of raw scores. The square root of this value is then divided by the number of cases to give the standard deviation. Note well that ΣX^2 is quite different from $(\Sigma X)^2$. If in a sample we have three raw scores, 3, 4 and 5, then $\Sigma X = (3 + 4 + 5) = 12$; $\Sigma X^2 = (3^2 + 4^2 + 5^2) = 50$ and $(\Sigma X)^2 = 12^2 = 144$.

The Standard Normal Distribution

In the normal (or Gaussian) distribution all three measures of central tendency, the mean, the mode and the median, fall exactly at the same point. This point is where the frequency, y in Fig. 7.1, is at its maximum.

Consider a variable such as height, which is essentially a normally distributed variable. This means that we can expect to find, on plotting the frequencies of various heights in a population of people, that while there are a few very tall people and a few very short people, most fall somewhere in the middle. The most frequently occurring height (the *mode*) will also be the point which divides the population into two equal groups (the *median*) as well as being the value which is the *mean*

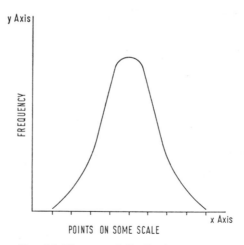

FIG. 7.1. The normal distribution curve.

height of the whole population. The curve of the distribution in Fig. 7.1 shows that the decrease in frequency is very marked at first then tapers off.

The mathematical equation defining the normal curve is such that we can calculate the frequency with which any score occurs in any population provided we know the size (N) of the population, its mean score and the standard deviation of the scores. Usually we convert the raw score into a deviation score (from the mean); if we want to know how many people in our population are 5 feet 11 inches tall when the mean height is 5 feet 8 inches, we ask "How many people are there at the point where the deviation from the mean is $+3$?"

The area under a curve varies with N, the size of the population or group under scrutiny, so that to find the absolute frequency of a value we would have to refer to the equation defining the curve every time. However, although the absolute frequency of a value varies with N, its *proportionate* frequency remains the same as can be seen in Fig. 7.2.

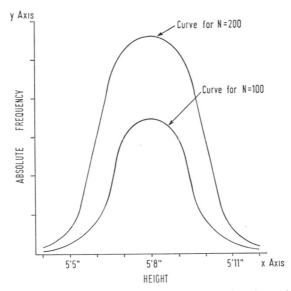

Fig. 7.2. Although the distributions differ in size they have the same proportions.

This matter of proportionate frequency can be illustrated by the familiar practice of turning examination or essay marks into percentages so that scores with different denominators can be compared. In such cases a score of 30 out of 60 becomes 50%, while one of 30 out of 50 becomes 60%. These percentages can be written $\frac{50}{100}$ and $\frac{60}{100}$ where we have set N at 100; they can also be written 0.50 and 0.60 if we set N at 1. In either case the changing of actual scores, with differing N, into proportionate scores helps us compare the two sets of examination marks.

In a similar way statisticians have dealt with the problem of handling frequencies where N varies. They have worked out all the frequency distribution values for a curve where $N = 1$, the standard deviation is also set at 1 and the mean score is at zero. If, looking at Fig. 7.1, we have on the horizontal axis (x) scores on a variable and on the vertical axis (y) a scale of frequency, then when $N = 1$ and s.d. $= 1$ we can read off for any score x (a deviation from the mean) a value of y, its frequency of occurrence. This value of y will be expressed as a proportion of N, the sample size, and since we have set $N = 1$, y will be a decimal figure. Table 1 of the *Cambridge Elementary Statistical Tables* is concerned with the normal distribution.

In order to use this *standard normal distribution* we have to transform the scores or values obtained in a given sample of cases with a particular mean and individual standard deviation into scores or deviations from a mean of zero with a standard deviation of unity. We have already used the transformation $x = X - \bar{x}$; that is a raw score (X) is transformed into a deviation score (x) so that the mean score of the population ($\bar{x}$) becomes zero. To calculate a standard score, or in full a standard deviation score, which we denote by z, we divide the deviation score (x) by the standard deviation of the sample.

Thus:

$$z = \frac{X - \bar{x}}{\text{s.d.}} = \frac{x}{\text{s.d.}} .$$

Consider the following example. A student obtains a mark of 68 in a sociology examination in which the class mean is 60 and the standard deviation of marks is 10.

(a) What is his x score; Deviation score $= X - \bar{x} = 68 - 60 = 8.$

(b) What is his z score; Standard score $= \dfrac{X - \bar{x}}{\text{s.d.}} = \dfrac{x}{\text{s.d.}} = \dfrac{8}{10} = 0.8.$

In the case where the standard deviation equals unity, $x = z$. A slightly more complicated example, but one which reflects a frequently occurring real life assessment situation, appears in Table 7.1.

TABLE 7.1. ASSESSMENT OF CLIENT DISABILITY BY SOCIAL WORKERS

Client	Social worker					Mean assessment for each client
	A	B	C	D	E	
Joe	49	55	50	50	66	54.0
Mick	61	53	58	42	58	54.4
Fred	55	52	56	52	64	55.8
Mary	48	47	56	40	60	50.2
John	58	56	56	46	60	55.2
Arthur	63	60	64	54	68	62.2
Bob	42	58	54	52	60	53.2
Linda	57	58	50	54	58	55.4
Sue	56	60	58	56	62	59.0
Carol	49	58	52	48	55	52.4
Mean	53.80	55.70	55.40	49.40	61.10	
Mode	49	58	56	52	60	
Median	55.5	57	56	51	60	
Standard deviation	6.24	3.87	4.00	3.60	3.75	

The table shows the proportionate physical disability of ten clients assessed by five social workers (A, B, C, D and E) where total disability is scored as 100.

An examination of Table 7.1 shows that the mean assessments for each client range from 50.2 to 62.2. The social workers show a great deal of variation in their average scores (using any or all of the three methods available). Social worker A has the lowest mean for her disability ratings (53.80), while social worker E has the highest (61.10). The standard deviations of the ratings of each worker also vary to a marked degree. These differences in the ratings given by individual social workers can be eliminated by transforming their ratings into

standard scores (z) using the formula already presented, i.e. $z = \dfrac{x.}{\text{s.d.}}$.
Table 7.2 shows how this is done for social worker A; the reader may find it profitable to carry out the calculations necessary to obtain z scores for social workers B, C, D and E.

TABLE 7.2. TRANSFORMING SCORES INTO STANDARD DEVIATION SCORES
Social Worker A

Client	Raw score assessment (X)	Deviation from mean (x)	Standard deviation scores (z)
Joe	49	−4.80	−0.769
Mick	61	7.20	1.153
Fred	55	1.20	0.192
Mary	48	−5.80	−0.929
John	58	4.20	0.673
Arthur	63	9.20	1.474
Bob	42	−11.80	−1.891
Linda	57	3.20	0.513
Sue	56	2.20	0.353
Carol	49	−4.80	−0.769
Mean	53.80		
Standard deviation	6.24		

It is inconvenient to work with z scores as they appear in Table 7.2, negative signs and decimal places are too often sources of error. An optional, but very useful, step is to change the z scores, which are deviation scores on a scale where the mean is set at zero and the standard deviation at unity, into scores on a scale where the mean and the standard deviation are set at some convenient figures. The most commonly used tests of adult intelligence use such a scale, the mean being set at 100 and the standard deviation at 15. Table 7.3 shows how to convert the z scores of Table 7.2 into a standard scale where we have arbitrarily set the mean at 100 and the standard deviation at 15. The formula for calculating each new standard scale score is:

Standard scale score $=$ mean $+$ (z times standard deviation)
$$= 100 + 15\,z.$$

TABLE 7.3. CHANGING *z* SCORES INTO STANDARD SCALE SCORES
Social Worker A

Client	Standard deviation score (z)	Standard* scale score	Rounded standard scale score
Joe	−0.769	88.465	88
Mick	1.153	117.295	117
Fred	0.192	102.880	103
Mary	−0.929	86.065	86
John	0.673	110.095	110
Arthur	1.474	122.110	122
Bob	−1.891	71.635	72
Linda	0.513	107.695	108
Sue	0.353	105.295	105
Carol	−0.769	88.465	88

* Mean set at 100, standard deviation set at 15.

It is not necessary to retain the decimal places when working with standard scale scores, the third column of Table 7.3 shows the whole-number, rounded standard scale scores which we would use in practice.

When we calculate standard scale scores for all five social workers we can compare the mean standard scale score which each client has with the mean of the raw scores given in Table 7.1. Table 7.4 shows the raw scores and the standard scale scores for all social workers.

The benefits of being able to transform raw scores into standard scale scores are evident in situations where many clients have to be assessed so that social worker A assesses and rates the first ten clients, worker B the next ten and so forth. Table 7.1 shows that social worker D tends to give lower scores than worker E, their mean scores differ by more than 10 points, although the dispersions about their respective means are similar. For social worker D, a raw score of 54, the score actually given to Linda, converts into a standard scale score of 119; for social worker E a raw score of 55, such as given to Carol, converts into a standard scale score of 76. The use of transformed scales can help to minimise differences in the assessment criteria of different workers and so facilitate the proper selection of those clients whose needs are greatest.

TABLE 7.4. RAW SCORES COMPARED WITH STANDARD SCALE SCORES

Client		Social worker											Mean	
	A		B		C		D		E					
	Raw	SSS	Raw	SSS	Raw	SSS	Raw	SSS	Raw	SSS			Raw	SSS
Joe	49	88	55	97	50	80	50	103	66	120			54.0	97.6
Mick	61	117	53	90	58	110	42	69	58	88			54.4	94.8
Fred	55	103	52	86	56	102	52	111	64	112			55.8	102.8
Mary	48	86	47	66	56	102	40	61	60	96			50.2	82.2
John	58	110	56	101	56	102	46	86	60	96			55.2	99.0
Arthur	63	122	60	117	64	132	54	119	68	128			62.2	123.6
Bob	42	72	58	109	54	95	52	111	60	96			53.2	96.6
Linda	57	108	58	109	50	80	54	119	58	88			55.4	100.8
Sue	56	105	60	117	58	110	56	127	62	104			59.0	112.6
Carol	49	88	58	109	52	87	48	94	55	76			52.4	90.8

Some Uses of Tables of the Normal Distribution Curve

Using tables calculated from the normal distribution it is possible to find, for any standard score (z), the frequency of occurrence (y) of such a score (Fig. 7.3). We can also find out other things such as the area under the curve between the mean and the standard score we are interested in and the area between the standard score and the tail of the curve. Look at Fig. 7.4, we must always remember that the normal curve is symmetrical so that the area under the curve between the mean and a standard score of say $+0.5$ is the same as the area between the mean and a standard score of -0.5. Now the total area under the curve is set at unity (since $N = 1$), so that knowing the area falling between two scores or values we can calculate what proportion of the total that area is and hence we can determine the proportionate number of cases or individuals lying between our two values.

Table 1 of the *Cambridge Tables* is so set out that for any deviation (x) from the mean, in a positive direction, the area between that deviation value and minus infinity is given. If we look for a deviation score of 1.00, that is one standard deviation from the mean, we read off a value of 0.8413. This signifies that 0.8413 of the area under the curve

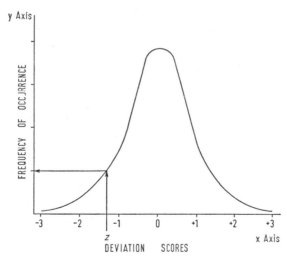

Fig. 7.3. Finding the frequency of occurrence of a standard score.

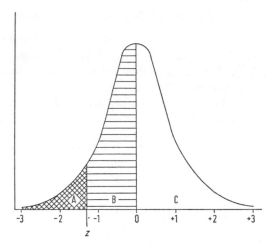

FIG. 7.4. Proportions of the area under the normal distribution curve.
A: Proportion of total area between 3 and minus infinity.
B: Proportion of total area between 3 and the mean.
C: Proportion of total area between the mean and plus infinity.

lies between minus infinity and $+1.00$ on the x axis. When $x = 0$, at the mid-point of the distribution, the area between that point and minus infinity is 0.5000. By subtraction we can calculate that the area under the curve between $x = 0$ and $x = 1.00$ is 0.3413. Note that in the *Cambridge Tables* x is used to denote the standard deviation scores which we have earlier denoted by z. If the reader remembers that in the *Cambridge Tables* x is a deviation score from a mean of zero where the standard deviation is unity he should avoid overmuch confusion. Between the deviation scores -1 and $+1$ lies 0.6826 of the total area under the curve. We can generalise this observation by saying that in any population considered on some measure or other, 68% of the cases or individuals involved will be found within the range of ± 1 standard deviation of the mean.

By considering the area under the curve between any chosen z score and the tail of the distribution, we can find how many cases or individuals have scores which exceed our chosen score. It is this feature of the normal curve which we use when applying "tests of significance" which are discussed later.

Recapitulation

A score or value by itself conveys no real information; if we go along a street and find out the weekly wage of each pedestrian we can say that John Smith has a wage of £40. This information will mean nothing unless we know how much other people earn. We use the notions of *central tendency* and *dispersion* to summarise what a group of people earn. We might express John Smith's earnings thus:

John Smith's wage	Central tendency of the group (mean)	Dispersion of wages in group
X £40	$x = \dfrac{X}{N}$ £45	s.d. $= \sqrt{\dfrac{x^2}{N}}$ £4

John Smith's earnings are £5 below the mean earnings for the group in question, in addition his earnings are outside the ± 1 s.d. (£41–£49) limits which include 68% of the group. The area between -1 s.d. and the lower tail of the normal curve is one-half of the difference between the total area minus the 68% included in the ± 1 s.d. range (the other half of the difference lies between $+1$ s.d. and the upper tail). We can say that with a weekly wage of £40 John Smith is in the bottom 16% of wage-earners in our group.

If we carry out a similar survey in another street we find that Tom Brown has a wage of £40 in a group whose mean earnings are £45 with a standard deviation of £7. Tom Brown's earnings are also £5 below the mean earnings of his group, but he is *inside* the ± 1 s.d. limits which include 68% of the group. Compared with their respective groups, Tom Brown is better off than John Smith.

It is clumsy to have to refer to a score in such a way that the mean and standard deviation have to be cited as well. Hence by the use of standard scores which allow direct comparisons: John Smith's standard score is -1.25, $\dfrac{(£40-£45)}{4}$, Tom Brown's is -0.71, $\dfrac{(£40-£45)}{7}$. Standard scores allow us to use to the full the properties of the normal distribution, and our earlier example made mention of some of them.

Reference

LINDLEY, D. V. and MILLER, J. C. P. (1966) *Cambridge Elementary Statistical Tables.* London: Cambridge University Press.

CHAPTER 8

Testing for Differences

A GREAT deal of data collection and research is centred around two aims: to find if a number of groups differ in respect of a certain characteristic or to find if a number of characteristics are related in the way in which they manifest themselves in a group. This chapter is concerned with testing for differences between groups. The questions posed are of the kind, "Are male clients older than female clients?", "Are clients living in high-rise housing more likely to present with child-rearing problems than clients living in conventional housing?", "Does social worker A spend more time than social worker B in dealing with similar casework referrals?" There are many different statistical procedures for testing differences of the kind quoted above. The choice of procedure will depend to a large extent on the nature of the data collected.

When our data constitute a sample or samples of observations which can be classified into separate categories or frequencies we can test the agreement, or lack of agreement, between the observed frequencies and the frequencies we might expect on some prior knowledge or some hypothetical ground. The statistic we use in this case is called χ^2 (Chi-square). Its formula is as follows:

$$\chi^2 = \sum \frac{(f_o - f_e)^2}{f_e}$$

where f_o is the *observed frequency of occurrence* of data in any one category and f_e is the *expected frequency of occurrence* in that same category. As we have indicated, our hypotheses usually state that there is no difference between the observed data and the chance expected frequencies. When the agreement between f_o and f_e is close, then the

111

difference $(f_o - f_e)$ will be small and so χ^2 will be small. When $(f_o - f_e)$ is large, then χ^2 will also be large. The larger χ^2 becomes, the more likely it is that the observed frequencies differ from the expected to a statistically significant degree.

Example of Chi-square (χ^2) in a One-sample Case

Suppose a social worker rates each of 600 children referred to her on a five-point scale for intelligence. Does the distribution of intelligence given by these ratings differ significantly from the gradings allocated using formal tests of intelligence? Table 8.1 shows the steps taken to calculate each $\dfrac{(f_o - f_e)^2}{f_e}$. When these are summed, we have the value $\chi^2 = 7.66$.

TABLE 8.1. EXAMPLE OF CHI-SQUARE IN A ONE-SAMPLE CASE

	Grade given					
	A	B	C	D	E	
Number allocated to each group by social worker	80	111	232	119	58	(f_o)
Number allocated to each group by I.Q. test	60	120	240	120	60	(f_e)
	20	−9	−1	−1	−2	$(f_o - f_e)$
	400	81	1	1	4	$(f_o - f_e)^2$
	6.67	0.68	0.27	0.01	0.03	$\left(\dfrac{f_o - f_e}{f_e}\right)^2$

Mathematicians have produced a number of curves for the chi-square statistic and the most useful values of these curves appear as Table 5 of the *Cambridge Tables*. In order to know which part of the table to use, we must establish the degrees of freedom (d.f.) which operate in any particular case. For χ^2 the rule is simple: d.f. $= (r-1)(c-1)$. Count the number of rows (r) in the table, count the number of columns (c), subtract 1 from each and multiply. A fuller explanation of degrees of freedom is given later in this chapter.

In the present example, d.f. $= (2-1)(5-1) = 4$. The table of values of χ^2 in the *Cambridge Tables* has degrees of freedom as its *rows* and selected percentage probability points as *columns*. Usually we are concerned with the columns to the right of the double vertical lines. Looking along the fourth row of figures (for 4 d.f.) we note that a χ^2 value of 7.78 would occur by chance 10 times in 100, a value of 9.49 would occur 5 times in 100 and so on. Our obtained value of 7.66 would occur by chance more than 10 times in 100. As has been stated earlier, when experimental figures are higher than those values which would occur by chance 5 times in 100 they are considered to be *statistically significant*. Our value of 7.66 does not even exceed the 10% level and so is not large enough to make us reject the null hypothesis; we must conclude that the two sets of gradings for intelligence do not differ.

Example of Chi-square (χ^2) in a Two-sample Case

A number of patients in a hospital ward are given a new drug while a comparable number of patients, similar to the others, are given the customary drug in a capsule which is identical to that containing the new preparation. After a month each patient is rated on a four-point scale of improvement. Do the two groups of patients in Table 8.2 differ significantly in the amount of improvement they show?

TABLE 8.2. COMPARING TWO GROUPS USING CHI-SQUARE

	Group 1	Group 2	Total
Very much better	7	1	8
Much better	30	19	49
Slightly better	51	63	114
Unchanged	22	17	39
Total	110	100	$N = 210$

All the values in Table 8.2 are *observed frequencies*. Unlike our previous example, there is no criterion set of frequencies against which to compare them. We prepare a set of theoretical *expected frequencies* from the marginal totals. This procedure rests on the assumption that, in this example where there were eight patients in the "Very much better" category, the groups under consideration do not differ, so that these eight patients could be expected to occur in Groups 1 and 2 in proportion to the total numbers in these groups. This is achieved by multiplying the marginal totals for any one category or cell and dividing the result by the grand total N. For the "Very much better" cell in Group 1 the f_e is $(110 \times 8) \div 210 = 4.19$; for the "Very much better" cell in Group 2 the f_e is $(100 \times 8) \div 210 = 3.81$, and so on for all the cells in turn.

For each cell of the table calculate "f_e", then "$f_o - f_e$", then "$(f_o - f_e)^2$" and lastly "$(f_o - f_e)^2 \div f_e$". Add up these final figures to get χ^2 which here equals 8.41. In our example we have 4 rows and 2 columns so that our d.f. $= (4 - 1)(2 - 1) = 3$. Referring to Table 5 of the *Cambridge Tables* we find that, for d.f. $= 3$, our obtained value of χ^2 is greater than the value delimiting the upper 5% of the distribution. We can say that there is a significant difference between the groups in their response to treatment.

The entries in Table 8.2 can be used to explain the notions of *degrees of freedom*. Consider row 1 ("Very much better" category). The total number of cases in this category is 8; if we then say that 7 of the cases come from Group 1 then the number of cases in Group 2 for this category is determined, since $8-7$ can only leave 1. So for row 1 we conclude that although it has two cells, one for each of the groups, only one of these cells has freedom to vary. Rows 2 and 3 have the same property. Row 4 has no freedom to vary at all; since the cell entries for column 1 must total 110 and we have entered 7, 30 and 51 in the preceding rows, the entry for row 4 of column 1 must be 22. Similarly the entry for row 4 of column 2 must be 17. It will be seen that the degrees of freedom equal 3, which is what we obtained with our rote formula.

In Table 8.2 it should be noted that Group 2 had only 1 person in the "Very much better" category. Chi-square gives distorted results when the *expected frequency* of any category or cell is small, usually defined as 5 or less. The occurrence of a very small *observed frequency* acts as a warning that the *expected frequency* might be small. If this proves to be so, then it is customary to combine the frequencies of two or more adjacent categories to raise the expected frequency to an acceptable level. Table 8.3 shows what happens to the values in Table 8.2 when we combine the "Very much better" and "Much better" categories.

TABLE 8.3. COMBINING CATEGORIES IN A TWO-SAMPLE TABLE

	Group 1	Group 2	Total
Very much better + Much better	37	20	57
Slightly better	51	63	114
Unchanged	22	17	39
Total	110	100	210

Our degrees of freedom are now 2, $\chi^2 = 6.50$, which is significant at the 5% level.

Chi-square in the 2 × 2 *Case*

Quite often in social research we find that bivariate tables are of the 2 × 2 variety, that is each of the two variables has two categories and the resulting table has 4 cells. In this case we can use another formula for χ^2, one which is quicker to calculate and which has a built-in correction for any distortions caused by small expected frequencies. Table 8.4 shows the layout of the bivariate table and the new formula.

Note that in this formula we take the absolute value of the expression $AD - BC$, ignoring the algebraic sign of the result.

TABLE 8.4. LAYOUT OF A 2 × 2 TABLE

A	B	(A + B)
C	D	(C + D)
(A + C)	(B + D)	N

$$\chi^2 = \frac{N[(AD - BC) - N/2]^2,}{(A + B)(C + D)(B + D)(A + C)}, \text{d.f.} = 1.$$

For example, a survey of suicide showed that a quarter of suicides had made a previous attempt to take their own lives. The question posed in Table 8.5 is, Did those suicides who had made a previous attempt use a different method to commit suicide compared with the rest of the group?

TABLE 8.5. EXAMPLE OF CHI-SQUARE IN A 2 × 2 TABLE

Method	Previous attempt	No previous attempt	Total
All except drugs	18	68	86
Drugs	31	79	110
Total	49	147	196

Applying the formula we get

$$\chi^2 = \frac{196[((18 \times 79) - (31 \times 68)) - 196/2]^2}{86 \times 110 \times 147 \times 49} = 0.99.$$

Looking at the table of χ^2 values for d.f. = 1 we see that for χ^2 to be significant at the 5% level (sometimes written 0.05 level) it must be greater than 3.84. In this example we conclude that a history of a previous attempt was not related to the method used to commit suicide.

The categories used in the above example are examples of discrete variables; one is a true dichotomy, the other a dichotomization of discrete categories. Individuals either did or did not have a known previous attempt and their methods of suicide could be correctly grouped into two categories, drugs and others. It is quite legitimate to combine categories in this way and it is also permissible to form dichotomies from data which are essentially continuous. For example, we could decide to call all ages from 15 to 44 years "young" and all those over 44 years "old".

The Accuracy of a Mean

Usually when we study some group of people we need to make some statement about the whole group, even though we have obtained our information from some fraction of the whole group. Public opinion polls provide a good example of this when they predict the voting intentions of a *population* (in this instance all those entitled to vote) from the stated intentions of a sample (a small proportion of the population). In statistical usage a *population* is some defined group of interest to the recorder, while a *sample* is a portion of the population. We assume that the findings we obtain in our *sample* will hold true for the whole *population*. Look back to page 85 where we had an example where we looked at the ages of new clients attending a social advice and welfare clinic. Our population would be all such new patients; our sample is those new patients who presented over a particular 2-week period. We might be asked "How sure are you that the average age obtained from this sample is an accurate measure of the average age of the whole population?" To answer this question we perform two calculations: first we calculate the *standard error* of our sample mean; next we apply our knowledge of the distribution of the normal curve to set up *confidence intervals* within which we can say that our sample mean coincides with the population mean.

The standard error of mean (s.e.) is calculated as follows:

$$\text{s.e.} = \frac{\text{s.d.}}{\sqrt{N}}$$

In the example quoted earlier we found a mean age of 32.6, a standard deviation of 11.8 and an N of 30. The standard error of this mean is found from $\frac{\text{s.d.}}{\sqrt{N}} = \frac{11.8}{\sqrt{30}} = 2.15$. If we had a sample which was much larger than the one used here we would have applied the z distribution to obtain the confidence limits of our mean. A z of 1.96 includes 95% of the area of the normal curve and so we could say with a 95% chance of being correct that the population mean would lie in the range covered by the mean plus or minus 1.96 times the standard error ($\bar{x} \pm 1.96$ s.e.).

Since our N is small, we must use a set of distributions which differ from the normal distribution in the values they demand for limits of confidence. The *t*-distribution, or set of distributions, has different values for different degrees of freedom where d.f. $= N - 1$. Table 3 of the *Cambridge Tables* has most of the figures the reader is likely to need in using the *t*-distribution. Like the table for χ^2, each *row* refers to a particular number of degrees of freedom while each *column* refers to a percentage point of the distribution. Consulting the table for d.f. $= 29$ we find that the value we need for the 95% confidence limit is 2.04. We apply our formula, $\bar{x} \pm 2.04$ s.e., to get values of 28.22 and 36.98. We can say that we are 95% confident that the true mean of the population from which our sample was drawn lies between 28.21 and 26.98 years.

It is obvious at a common sense level that the larger the size of the sample the more likely it is that the persons in the sample will be representative of the persons in the population as a whole. If in our sample we assume that the mean of 32.6 and the standard deviation of 11.8 had occurred in a sample of $N = 300$ instead of $N = 30$, we would have had a standard error of $\dfrac{\text{s.d.}}{\sqrt{N}} = \dfrac{11.8}{\sqrt{300}} = 0.68$. For d.f. $= 299$ we find that the value for the 95% confidence limit is 1.97. Applying the formula $\bar{x} \pm 1.97$ s.e., we obtain values of 31.26 and 33.94. The range between the upper and lower bounds of our confidence limits has been reduced from 8.76 to 2.68.

Comparing Two Means from Independent Samples

Consider a situation which could be related to our Example 2 hypothesis which stated: "There will be no differences in the number of cases which present at a social work agency according to the day of the week."

Related to the study which included this hypothesis, it might be important to look at the workload of the social workers involved. Two social workers, A and B, are allocated clients at random from the population who visit the agency. They are seen to differ in the number of interviews given to each client. Social worker A, with 95 clients, had a mean interviewing rate of 5.2, with a standard deviation of 1.8, while social worker B, with 90 clients, had a mean rate of 3.6, standard deviation 2.7. We wish to find out if the difference between the two means is a non-chance event. The formula for this procedure is:

$$z = \frac{\bar{x}_A - \bar{x}_B}{\sqrt{\dfrac{\text{s.d.}_A^2}{N_A} + \dfrac{\text{s.d.}_B^2}{N_B}}}$$

where z is the familiar standard deviation score, $\bar{x}_A$ is the mean value for social worker A and $\bar{x}_B$ is the mean value for social worker B. The letters A and B identify the various means, standard deviations and sample size. The bottom line of the formula enclosed by the square root sign takes the dispersion of the two distributions A and B into account and provides an estimate of the standard error of the difference between the two means. Dividing the difference between the two means by the standard error gives us a z score which we can refer to the normal distribution.

In this case the formula takes the following values:

$$z = \frac{5.2 - 3.6}{\sqrt{\dfrac{(1.8)^2}{95} + \dfrac{(2.7)^2}{90}}} = 4.72.$$

Before consulting Table 2 of the *Cambridge Tables* the reader should note that where no prediction has been made about differences, in other words it was not predicted before data collection took place that social worker A would have a higher interviewing rate than social worker B, then the probability points of the distribution have to be doubled. Thus, in the columns of Table 2 furthest to the right the x value (or z value is our terminology) of 1.9600, which is associated with the 2.5% probability level, is associated with the 5% level. This is because the z value could be either a positive or a negative deviation from the mean and the value of 1.9600 could relate to the extreme tails of the normal distribution at either the positive or negative end of the distribution. The convention has arisen that the value of 1.9600 is associated with the 2.5% zone at *each* end of the distribution, these adding to 5%.

Our obtained z value of 4.72 is greater than that associated with a p level of 0.0005 in Table 2, which when doubled gives us a probability level of 0.001%. This value of z would occur by chance less than once in one thousand cases, so we would be well justified statistically in considering that there was a real difference in the interviewing rates of the two social workers.

Where our samples are rather small, in practice where $(N_1 + N_2)$ is less than 60, we must use the formula based on the t-distributions mentioned earlier. If social worker A had only 25 clients and social worker B had 30, then we would have to use the following formula:

$$\bar{x} = \bar{x}_A - \bar{x}_B$$

$$t = \frac{\bar{x} = \bar{x}_A - \bar{x}_B}{\sqrt{\left[\frac{(N_A \times s.d._A^2) + (N_B \times s.d._B^2)}{(N_A + N_B - 2)}\right]\left(\frac{1}{N_A} + \frac{1}{N_B}\right)}}$$

$$= \frac{5.2 - 3.6}{\sqrt{\left[\frac{(25 \times 1.8^2) + (30 \times 2.7^2)}{(25 + 30 - 2)}\right]\left(\frac{1}{25} + \frac{1}{30}\right)}}$$

$$= 2.49.$$

For each sample, in this case A and B, we have calculated a mean score, thus losing one degree of freedom. Consequently we consult the table of the t-distribution at the point d.f. $= [(N_A - 1) + (N_B - 1)]$ which is $(25-1) + (30-1) = 53$, and find that a value of 2.49 would occur only twice in one hundred cases, so we could again conclude that the difference between the two social workers was a real one.

The t-test is probably the most common test of differences applied to continuously distributed data. In the t-test we can see that the significance of the difference between two sample means depends partly on the size of the samples and partly on the amount of variability or variance of scores in each sample. We have seen how the accuracy of a mean is influenced by the dispersion of scores about that mean; again *variance* has an important role to play.

Elementary Analysis of Variance

If we had a situation where we wished to compare mean differences between more than two groups we could not legitimately use the t-test. We would have to use another method called *analysis of variance*. This term embraces a whole range of statistical procedures, many of which are exceedingly complex but all of which depend on comparisons between the variability or variance present in different groups of subjects or objects.

Let us consider the following example. A sample of the ages of single, married and divorced or widowed clients in our Example hypothesis 2 attending an agency appear in Table 8.6.

We have shown earlier that it is useful to work with raw scores rather than deviation scores so as to avoid negative values and fractions. Where X is an observed value, age in this example, and X^2 is the square of such a value, we calculate the mean by

$$\bar{x} = \frac{\Sigma X}{N}$$

and the *sum of squares* by

$$\Sigma x^2 = \Sigma X^2 - \frac{(\Sigma X)^2}{N}.$$

The sum of squares divided by N, the number of cases, gives the *variance*, which is $\dfrac{\Sigma x^2}{N}$, or the standard deviation squared (s.d.^{2}).

TABLE 8.6. EXAMPLE OF ANALYSIS OF VARIANCE

	Group 1 Single	Group 2 Married	Group 3 Divorced/Widowed
	19	40	22
	20	35	60
	19	21	59
	30	27	44
	22	36	51
	25	50	
		41	
$n =$	6	7	5
$\Sigma X =$	135	250	236
$\Sigma X^2 =$	3131	9472	12,102

$\Sigma(\Sigma X) = $ Grand total $\Sigma(\Sigma X^2) = $ Grand sum of squared values $= 24,705$
$= 621\ (135 + 250 + 236)$ $(3131 + 9472 + 12,102)$
$N = (6 + 7 + 5) = 18$

Looking at Table 8.6 we can see that the Grand total can be obtained by adding each age score together or by adding them for each group first and then adding the three ΣX values; hence $\Sigma(\Sigma X)$. Similarly the Grand sum of squared values can be obtained directly for the whole group or by first finding the sum of squared raw values for each group and then adding the three ΣX^2 values; hence $\Sigma(\Sigma X^2)$.

We will denote the size of the whole sample by N, using n_1, n_2, n_3 to denote the sizes of each of the three groups. The same letters or subscripts will be used to identify the appropriate ΣX and ΣX^2 values.

The mean of the whole sample is:

$$\bar{x} = \frac{\Sigma(\Sigma X)}{N} = \frac{621}{18} = 34.50.$$

The sum of squares of the deviations of all scores from the mean of the whole sample (the Total sum of squares) is:

$$\Sigma x^2 = \Sigma(\Sigma X^2) - \frac{\Sigma(\Sigma X)^2}{N} = 24{,}705 - \frac{621^2}{18} = 3280.50.$$

This Total sum of squares shown in Table 8.7 can be broken up or *partitioned* into *two sources of variance*. One source is termed variance between the groups and can be recognised if we think of the mean scores of the groups being like the scores in Fig. 6.5 (page 93) so that the grand mean $[\Sigma(\Sigma X)]$ is the point of balance between them. We would calculate the sum of squares of these values about the mean by summing the square of each group mean's deviation from the grand mean, thus $(\bar{x}_1 - \text{grand mean})^2 + (\bar{x}_2 - \text{grand mean})^2 + (\bar{x}_3 - \text{grand mean})^2$, which in raw score terminology becomes

$$\frac{(\Sigma X_1)^2}{n_1} + \frac{(\Sigma X_2)^2}{n_2} + \frac{(\Sigma X_3)^2}{n_3} - \frac{[\Sigma(\Sigma X)]^2}{N}.$$

In this example our Between groups sum of squares is:

$$\frac{135^2}{6} + \frac{250^2}{7} + \frac{236^2}{5} = \frac{621^2}{18} = 1680.77.$$

Our remaining source of variance in this example is the variance *within each group* which we represent by the sum of squares of deviation of scores around each group mean. For each group we calculate $\Sigma X^2 - \left(\dfrac{\Sigma X}{N}\right)^2$, which gives us as our Within groups sum of squares:

$$\left(3131 - \frac{135^2}{6}\right) + \left(9472 - \frac{250^2}{7}\right) + \left(12,102 - \frac{236^2}{5}\right) = 1599.73.$$

Note well that the variance *within* groups added to the variance *between* groups reproduces the *total variance* as measured by the total sum of squares. This is a key aspect of analysis of variance. The variance from different sources are additive.

Our calculations may be set out as in Table 8.7.

TABLE 8.7. SUMMARY OF ANALYSIS OF VARIANCE

Source of sums of squares	d.f.	Sums of squares	Variance (sums of squares ÷ d.f.)	F ratio
Total group	$(N - 1) = 17$	3280.50		
Between groups	$(\text{groups} - 1) = 2$	1680.77	840.38	7.88
Within groups	$(n_1 - 1) + (n_2 - 1) + (n_3 - 1) = 15$	1599.73	106.65	$(p < 0.001)$

Column 3 gives two estimates of the variance of the whole group. The within group variance, since it is based on the pooled sums of squares of each of the three groups studied, is used as the overall variance or index of variability for the total group. The between group variance reflects the degree to which the means of the individual groups are scattered about the grand mean. Where the difference between means is small, the between group variance will be small; where large, then the variance will be large. If the differences between means are due to random factors, then these random factors will also be present within the groups and the two variance estimates will be very similar, their *ratio* will approximate 1:1. The greater the ratio of the between group variance to the within group variance, the greater the likelihood that the differences between the group means are significant. This is called the *F ratio*. Tables of this ratio have been calculated for various probability levels and these form Table 7 of the *Cambridge Tables*.

Our degrees of freedom are 2 for between groups and 15 for within groups. Looking at column 2 row 15 of the *F* distribution, we find that a *F* ratio of 7.88 would occur less than once in one hundred cases. We can conclude that there is a difference between the mean ages of our three groups.

Presenting the Results of t-*tests and Analysis of Variance*

In presenting the results of a *t*-test one must *always* present the *t*-value and the degrees of freedom. It is not enough to present the probability value alone. Using the results of the example, we would write: "The difference in mean number of interviews per client by the two social workers was statistically significant ($t = 2.49$, d.f. $= 53$, $p < 0.02$)."

For the analysis of variance it is customary to present a summary table such as Table 8.7. This is very necessary when complicated analyses are being reported. The one-way analysis of variance set out here could be presented rather like a *t*-test result with "$F, (2, 15) = 7.88, p < 0.001$" being an acceptable format. This would be a convenient method of presentation where a great many one-way analyses were being reported.

CHAPTER 9

Testing for Relationships—Correlation and Partial Correlation

IN almost any branch of the behavioural or social sciences there is a search for variables which "go together" in such a way that changes in variable A are accompanied by changes in variable B. There is a constant striving in these sciences to reduce the complexity of the phenomena being studied, for instance most research in a given area begins with surveys which, suitably analysed, highlight the relevance of some items and allow us to discard other items as being less relevant. Such a procedure reduces the number of variables which have to be considered in further studies. Sometimes this procedure is carried out without any formal statistical analysis, at other times tests such as the χ^2 test are used. Where the researcher is looking for variables which are related to the variable in which he is interested, then some index of *correlation* is the most frequently used statistical method.

All indices of correlation describe the degree of association between two variables, they provide in a single set of figures a way of describing to what extent variations in one item change along with variations in the other. In the social sciences there are very few variables which are perfectly related. It is hard to think of a situation where if variable A is always present then variable B is always present. More likely is the situation where if variable A is always present then variable B is frequently present. An index of correlation will describe in a quantified manner the extent of "frequently". Most measures of correlation range from $+1$, which indicates perfect positive association between variables, through 0, indicating the complete absence of association, to -1 which indicates perfect negative association.

It must be stated very clearly that *correlation does not of itself imply causation.* While variables *A* and *B* might correlate very highly indeed, we cannot, on the basis of the correlation index alone, say anything about *A* causing *B* or vice versa.

Product–Moment Correlation

We will now present some of the methods which are used to establish the extent of correlations between variables.

The most frequently used index of correlation is the product-moment *correlation coefficient,* denoted by *r.* In mathematical language deviations about a mean are termed "moments". As has been shown earlier, standard scores (z) are deviates about a mean of zero, they are the *first moments* of the distribution (squared deviations are second moments, cubed deviations third moments and so on). The relationship between two variables, expressed as the coefficient *r,* is the average product of the first moments of the standard deviation score distributions of the two variables.

The basic formula for *r* is:

$$r = \frac{\Sigma\, z_1\, z_2,}{N}$$

where *r* denotes the correlation coefficient, Σ is the "sum of all", z_1 is a standard deviation score for a person on variable 1, z_2 is a standard deviation score for that same person on variable 2 and *N* is the number of cases or persons involved.

The reader may recall from Chapter 7 (Tables 7.1 and 7.2) that a number of social workers assessed the proportionate physical disability of ten clients. From these assessments some simple statistics were calculated, mean, mode and median as well as some measures of dispersion, deviation from the mean and standard deviation. Using the same data, Table 9.1 goes on to examine the degree of correlation between the scores given to each client by social workers A and B. This is done to find out the extent of the variations between their independent assessments. In other words, are the two social workers overall assessing the same clients in a like manner?

TABLE 9.1. CALCULATING *r* FROM STANDARD SCORES

Client	Social Worker A (z_1)	Social Worker B (z_2)	$z_1 \times z_2$
Joe	−0.769	−0.181	0.139
Mick	1.154	−0.698	−0.805
Fred	0.192	−0.956	−0.183
Mary	0.930	−2.248	2.090
John	0.673	0.078	0.052
Arthur	1.474	1.111	1.637
Bob	−1.891	0.594	−1.123
Linda	0.513	0.594	0.304
Sue	0.353	1.111	0.392
Carol	−0.769	0.594	−0.456
$N = 10$			$\Sigma z_1 z_2 = 2.047$

$$r = \frac{\Sigma z_1 z_2}{N} = \frac{2.047}{10} = 0.2047 \text{ or } 0.205 \text{ (to 3 decimal places).}$$

In earlier chapters we have shown how standard deviation scores are derived from deviation scores and ultimately from the raw scores on a test or other variable. Given this knowledge it is possible to expand the basic formula to deal with deviation scores, thus:

$$r = \frac{\Sigma x y}{\sqrt{(\Sigma x^2) (\Sigma y^2)}}$$

or with raw scores, when the formula becomes:

$$r = \frac{N \Sigma X Y - (\Sigma X)(\Sigma Y)}{\sqrt{[N \Sigma X^2 - (\Sigma X)^2] [N \Sigma Y^2 - (\Sigma Y)^2]}}.$$

The 'raw score' formula for calculating a correlation coefficient is the one which the majority of readers will use when they have access to a desk calculator. In most research the means and standard deviations of variables are almost always required so that for variables X and Y the terms ΣX, ΣX^2, ΣY and ΣY^2 will be available, leaving $\Sigma X Y$ as the only additional term to be calculated before applying the correlation formula. Applying the raw score formula to columns A and B of Table 7.1 yields the coefficient $r = 0.204$. The very slight discrepancy between the correlations obtained using different formulae is due to accumulated errors which occur when figures are rounded off to a set number of decimal places.

Having obtained a correlation coefficient, we want to interpret it. First of all we want to know if it is statistically significant and we approach this in the same way that we asked whether two means were significantly different. We use the formula:

$$t = \frac{r\sqrt{N-2}}{\sqrt{1-r^2}},$$

with d.f. $= N - 2$. In calculating the two sets of standard scores from which r was calculated, two means were calculated and hence 2 degrees of freedom are lost. In the present case we have:

$$t = \frac{0.204 \sqrt{10-2}}{\sqrt{1 - (0.204)^2}} = 0.589.$$

Consulting Table 3 of the *Cambridge Tables* we find that for 8 degrees of freedom the expected value of t at the 5% level is 2.31; our coefficient does not differ significantly from zero.

The reader should note that the size of the sample from which the correlation was derived is important, since not only does it determine the degrees of freedom but also influences the value of t by appearing in the denominator. If our correlation of 0.204 has been obtained on a sample of 90 persons, then the value of t would have been 1.954 which is just short of the expected value of 1.987 for 88 d.f. Had the sample numbered 100, then t would have equalled 2.063 and the correlation would have been significant at the 5% level of confidence. This is yet another example of the need to have adequate sampling of any population. In general, the larger the sample the more likely it is to be representative of the population from which it is drawn.

The Spearman Rank Order Correlation Coefficient

There are a number of correlation coefficients which derive from the product–moment formula and can be considered as special cases of the latter. For the social scientist the most useful of these is the Spearman rank order correlation coefficient rho (denoted r_s) which is an index of correlation which uses the rank order of variables as a basis for computation. Although it looks quite different from the product–moment formula, it is in fact a special case of *r*. The formula for rho is:—

$$r_s = 1 - 6\Sigma d^2/(N^3 - N)$$

where N is the number of cases ranked and d is the difference in ranks between each pair of observations. As an example let us look again at the first two columns of Table 7.1. If we take the raw scores given by social worker A and give a rank of 1 to Arthur who has the highest score, a rank of 2 to Mick who has the next highest score and so on, we produce a set of rankings which reflects the relative positions of the clients as assessed by A. Table 9.2 shows the raw scores and the rankings for social workers A and B. In ranking column A we find that Joe and Carol have the same raw score (49), they share the rank positions 7 and 8 which we enter as 7.5 for each client. The next rank, for Mary whose raw score is 48, is 9. In ranking column B we find Arthur and Sue tie for ranks 1 and 2, thus each is ranked 1.5, while the three clients Bob, Linda and Carol share the next three ranks 3, 4 and 5.

TABLE 9.2. CALCULATING A RHO CORRELATION COEFFICIENT

| Client | Raw scores | | Ranks | | | |
	Social Worker A	Social Worker B	*A*	*B*	*d*	*d²*
Joe	49	55	7.5	7	0.5	0.25
Mick	61	53	2	8	6	36
Fred	55	52	6	9	3	9
Mary	48	47	9	10	1	1
John	58	56	3	6	3	9
Arthur	63	60	1	1.5	0.5	0.25
Bob	42	58	10	4	6	36
Linda	57	58	4	4	0	0
Sue	56	60	5	1.5	3.5	12.25
Carol	49	58	7.5	4	3.5	12.25

$$\Sigma d^2 = 116$$

$$r_s = 1 - \left(\frac{6\Sigma d^2}{N^3 - N}\right) = 1 - \left(\frac{6 \times 116}{1000 - 10}\right) = 1 - \frac{696}{990} = 0.297.$$

Each is given the middle rank 4 and the next highest scorer, John, is given rank 6. When ties occur, the cases which tie are given a rank which is the mid-point of the number of tied cases. Column *d* shows the diff-erences between pairs of rankings, each *d* being squared and the squares added. The rho correlation is larger than that obtained using the product–moment formula.

Where tied ranks occur, it is advisable to introduce a correction for these ties. The formula then becomes:

$$r_s = \frac{\Sigma x^2 \, \Sigma y^2 - \Sigma d^2}{2\sqrt{\Sigma x^2 \, \Sigma y^2}}$$

where $x^2 = \left(\dfrac{N^3 - N}{12} - \Sigma Tx\right)$ and $\Sigma y^2 = \left(\dfrac{N^3 - N}{12} - \Sigma Ty\right)$,

ΣTx and ΣTy being the corrections for tied ranks in the two variables being correlated. Each value of T is calculated by $T = \dfrac{t^3 - t}{12}$ where t is the number of observations tied at a given rank.

In our example, letting x denote the values for social worker **A** and y those for social worker **B**, we find that $\Sigma Tx = \left(\dfrac{2^3 - 2}{10}\right) = 0.6$, there being one set of tied ranks involving 2 cases, $\Sigma Ty = \left(\dfrac{2^3 - 2}{10}\right) + \left(\dfrac{3^3 - 3}{10}\right)$ $= 3$, there being two sets of tied ranks, one involving 2 cases, the other involving 3 cases. Substituting these values we find that $\Sigma x^2 = \dfrac{10^3 - 10}{12}$ $- 0.6 = 81.9$ and $\Sigma y^2 = \dfrac{10^3 - 10}{12} - 3 = 79.5$. When these figures are inserted into the expanded formula we get:

$$r_s = \frac{81.9 + 79.5 - 116}{2\sqrt{81.9 \times 79.5}} = \frac{45.400}{161.382} = 0.281.$$

With only a few ties the effect of correction is small; where many ties are present then failure to correct could produce distorted values of rho.

The significance of a rho coefficient is tested in the same way as is a product moment coefficient:

$$t = \frac{r_s \sqrt{N-2}}{\sqrt{1-r_s^2}} \text{ with d.f.} = 2, \text{ which is } \frac{0.281 \sqrt{8}}{\sqrt{1-(0.281)^2}}$$

$$= \frac{0.281 \times 2.828}{0.96} = 0.828.$$

Thus, using our r_s which is corrected for ties we obtain a t value of 0.828 which is not statistically significant.

The rho coefficient is most appropriately used when the variables being correlated are adequately expressed as ranks. If, in the example we have been using, the social workers had been asked at the outset to rank the clients from the most to the least disabled, then r_s would have been the best choice of correlation coefficient. However, because r_s is derived from r, we find little difference between the two indices. If we apply the product–moment formula to Table 9.2, treating the *ranks* as if they were raw scores, then we find $r = 0.284$.

Often r_s is used as a short-cut approximation to r at some preliminary stage in an investigation. Since this use is approximate it is usual to ignore tied ranks and to use the formula $r_s = 1 - \dfrac{6\Sigma d^2}{N^3 - N}$. As the availability of desk calculations and computers increases, so the need to use 'short-cut' methods in statistics grows less.

The Kendall Rank Order Correlation Coefficient

For most purposes, the reader of this book will find r_s the most useful coefficient to apply to data such as the example we have been using. There are occasions, however, where the number of cases to be ranked is very large and the number of ranks is curtailed, as in a rating scale, so that some other measure of correlation is sought. Kendall's correlation coefficient tau (τ) is useful in such cases. While not restricted to the kinds of problem to be demonstrated here, it is in such instances that it is most valuable.

Table 9.3 presents the rank ordering of clients which we calculated in Table 9.2. The main difference is that the order in which the clients are listed has been altered to correspond with their ranks on A. If there were perfect agreement between social workers A and B, their rank orders would be identical so that working from left to right along row B each rank would be in the correct order of precedence when compared with its neighbours. The extent to which the rank order of row B departs from that of row A provides the basis for calculating tau which we can write thus:

$$\tau = \frac{S}{\frac{1}{2}N\,(-1)},$$

where N is the number of cases and S is a figure found by comparing all pairs of ranks in row B assigning $+1$ to each case where a pair are in their correct, "natural order", a score of 0 when a pair have the same rank and a score of -1 when a pair are in reversed order. The third row of Table 9.3 shows that as rated by social worker B, Arthur's rank position relative to Mick, John, and Linda is correct, he ranks above each; he ties with Sue, and ranks higher than Fred, Joe, Carol, Mary and Bob. Mick ranks below John, Linda and Sue, is above Fred, is below Joe and Carol, above Mary and below Bob. These pairs of comparisons are continued until the last row indicates that Mary's rank is lower than that of Bob.

In our example the total of these comparisons is 24 natural order pairs. 4 ties and 17 reverse order pairs, i.e. $+7$. Entering this value of S into the formula, we find that $\tau = 0.156$. As with r_s we must correct the formula for τ when tied ranks are present. The corrected formula is:

$$\tau = \frac{S}{\sqrt{[\frac{1}{2}N\,(N-1) - T]\,[\frac{1}{2}N\,(N-1) - U]}},$$

where T and U are found by $\frac{1}{2}\,\Sigma\,t\,(t-1)$, and $\frac{1}{2}\,\Sigma\,u\,(u-1)$ respectively, t and u being the number of tied observations in each group of ties on the appropriate variable. In this case, letting T represent row A (the ranks of worker A) and U row B (the ranks of worker B) we get:

TABLE 9.3. CALCULATING A TAU CORRELATION COEFFICIENT

Client

	Arthur	Mick	John	Linda	Sue	Fred	Joe	Carol	Mary	Bob
Ranks for social worker A	1	2	3	4	5	6	7.5	7.5	9	10
Ranks for social worker B	1.5	8	6	4	1.5	9	7	4	10	4
Arthur		+1	+1	+1	0	+1	+1	+1	+1	+1
Mick			−1	−1	−1	+1	−1	−1	+1	−1
John				−1	−1	+1	+1	−1	+1	−1
Linda					−1	+1	+1	0	+1	0
Sue						+1	+1	+1	+1	+1
Fred							−1	−1	+1	−1
Joe								−1	+1	−1
Carol									+1	0
Mary										−1

Comparing pairs of ranks

$$\tau = \frac{S}{\frac{1}{2}N(N-1)}$$

$$= \frac{24 - 17}{\frac{1}{2}(10)(9)}$$

$$= \frac{+7}{45}$$

$$= 0.156.$$

$$T = \tfrac{1}{2} (2 (2 - 1)) = 1,$$

$$U = \tfrac{1}{2} (2 (2 - 1)) + (3 (3 - 1)) = 4$$

and

$$\tau = \frac{+7}{\sqrt{45 - 1} \; \sqrt{45 - 4}} = 0.165.$$

The significance of τ is found by reference to the normal distribution since when the number of cases is greater than 8 the sampling distribution of S, and hence t, is practically indistinguishable from that of z. Kendall prefers to calculate the significance of S rather than τ itself; the formula where no ties are present is:—

$$z = \frac{|S| - 1}{\sigma_s} = \frac{|S| - 1}{\dfrac{\sqrt{N(N - 1) (2N + 5)}}{18}}$$

The absolute value of S is reduced by 1, $(|S| - 1)$, thus correcting for continuity. The probability of the obtained value of z occurring by chance is read off from the normal distribution table in the way described on page 107, doubling the p level. Where tied ranks occur, it is necessary to correct the standard deviation which otherwise would fall below its true value. This leads to a very long formula for the denominator which is presented here in its squared form, i.e. for σ_s^2, to avoid the further complication of the square root sign. The formula for σ_s^2 is as follows:

$$\sigma_s^2 = 1/18 \; [N (N - 1) (2N + 5) - \Sigma t (t - 1) (2t + 5) - \Sigma u (u - 1) (2u + 5)]$$

$$+ \frac{1}{9N (N - 1) (N - 2)} \; [\Sigma t (t - 1) (t - 2)] \; [\Sigma u (u - 1) (u - 2)]$$

$$+ \frac{1}{2N (N - 1)} \; [\Sigma t (t - 1)] \; [\Sigma u (u - 1)].$$

Parts of this formula, e.g. $\tfrac{1}{18}$, are given constants derived from mathematical proofs. In our example we can write out the formula as follows:

$$\sigma_s^2 = \tfrac{1}{18} \; [(10) \; (9) \; (25) - (2) \; (1) \; (9) - (2) \; (1) \; (9) + (3) \; (2) \; (11)]$$

$$+ \frac{1}{9 \ (10) \ (9) \ (8)} \ [2 \ (1) \ (0)] \ \{[2 \ (1) \ (0)] + [3 \ (2) \ (1)]\}$$

$$+ \frac{1}{2 \ (10) \ (9)} \ [2 \ (1)] \ \{[2 \ (11) + 3 \ (2)]\}$$

$$= 122.91.$$

The reader should note from this example that although the formula is formidable in length, it is very easily calculated in practice.

Note that t, referring to the tie which occurs for row A of Table 9.3, has fewer bracketed steps than u, which refers to the two sets of ties for row B. The values for these latter ties have to be calculated and then added before working outside the brackets in the formula.

The square root of 122.91 is 11.08. Dividing $|S| - 1$ by this value yields a z of 0.54, which is not statistically significant.

Where only one or two ties are present in the data, the effect of correcting for ties is very small and for many purposes can be ignored. However, the next example is of a situation where tau is a very useful index of correlation and where there are a great many ties. In this situation the corrected formula must be used to avoid obtaining inflated τ values and hence spuriously significant results.

Kendall's τ in Contingency Tables

Seventy-nine candidates were interviewed by a social worker with a view to becoming a member of the Samaritans. Each candidate was rated on a three-point scale on a number of relevant variables including the presence of personality problems. The social worker's overall rating of each candidates' potential as a Samaritan was on a five-point scale. Table 9.4 presents these two rating scales in the form of a contingency table.

If we look at the sum of each row we see that 34 candidates were rated 'definitely absent" with regard to the presence of personality problems, 29 were rated "possibly present" and the remaining 16 "definitely present". In other words the 34 were all seen as ranking better than the 29 who in turn were ranked better than the 16. For the first rank there is a tie of 34 cases, for the next rank a tie of 29 and for

TABLE 9.4. KENDALL'S τ IN A CONTINGENCY TABLE

Personality problems	Potential as a Samaritan					Sum of rows
	Very good	Good	Not sure	Poor	Very poor	
Definitely absent	19	13	2	0	0	34
Possibly present	0	10	12	7	0	29
Definitely present	0	0	0	9	7	16
Sum of columns	19	23	14	16	7	79 = N

the third a tie of 16. A similar state of affairs holds for the rating of potential as a Samaritan.

In a contingency table such as we have in Table 9.4 we calculate S in a manner which differs from that spelled out before, although the principle is the same. There will be a positive contribution to S from the product of each cell in the table and the sum of all the cells below and to the right of it. There will be a negative contribution from the product of each cell and the sum of all the cells below and to the left of it.

From the figures in Table 9.4 we calculate S as follows:

$S = 19 (10 + 12 + 7 + 9 + 7)$ plus $13 (12 + 7 + 9 + 7)$ plus 2 $(7 + 9 + 7)$ plus $10 (9 + 7)$ plus $12 (9 + 7)$ plus $7 (7)$ minus $2 (10)$,

$S = 1737.$

Now the formula for τ in the contingency case is:

$$\tau = \frac{2S}{N^2 \left(\dfrac{m - 1}{m} \right)},$$

where S is the index of disarray, N is the size of the sample and m is the number of rows or columns in the table, whichever is the smaller. In our example we have 3 rows and 5 columns, so $m = 3$.

Substituting our value we get:

$$\tau = \frac{2 (1737)}{79^2 (2/3)} = \frac{3474}{4160.66} = 0.835.$$

In practical work with contingency tables it is always the case that both variables have tied ranks. It would be possible to create a table with only one entry per row and column, but this would be uncommon, so we always apply the corrected formula for calculating the standard deviation of S. Taking the formula step by step we calculate:

$1/18 [N (N - 1) (2N + 5)] = 1/18 [79 (78) (163)]$, N being the total number of cases,

$-\Sigma t (t - 1) (2t + 5) = [34 (33) (73)] + [29 (28) (63)] + [16 (15) (37)]$ there being one tie of 34 cases, one of 29 cases and one of 16 cases,

$-\Sigma u (u - 1) (2u + 5) = [19 (18) (43)] + [23 (22) (51)] + [14 (13) (33)] + [16 (15) (37)] + [7 (6) (19)]$, there being one tie of 19 cases, one of 23, one of 14, one of 16 and one of 7 cases.

This first part of the formula yields the value

$$\frac{1,004,606 - 141,942 - 56,196}{18} = 44,792.66.$$

The next part we write as follows:

$\Sigma t (t - 1) (t - 2) = [34 (33) (32)] + [29 (28) (27)] + [16 (15) (14)]$,

$\Sigma u (u - 1) (u - 2) = [19 (18) (17)] = [23 (22) (21)] + [14 (13) (12)] +$

$[16 (15) (14)] + [7 (6) (5)]$

$9N (N - 1) (N - 2) = 9 (79) (78) (77)$.

This second part gives the value:

$$\frac{(61,188) (22,194)}{4,270,266} = 318.01.$$

Lastly we have:

$\Sigma t (t - 1) = [34 (33)] + [29 (28)] + [16 (15)]$

$\Sigma u (u - 1) = [19 (18)] + [23 (22)] + [14 (13)] + [16 (15)] + [7 (6)]$

$2N (N - 1) = 2 (79) (78)$,

which gives the value: $\dfrac{(2174)\,(1312)}{12{,}324} = 231.44.$

Thus $\sigma_s{}^2 = 44{,}792.66 + 318.01 + 231.44$

$\qquad\quad = 45{,}342.11,$

and $\sigma_s = 212.93$

$$z = \frac{|S| - 1}{\sigma_s}$$

$$= \frac{1737 - 1}{212.93}$$

$$= 8.15.$$

Consulting Table 2 of the *Cambridge Tables*, remembering to double the *p* values since we are taking account of chance at both tails of the distribution (hence the description 'two-tail test' applied to this procedure), we find that a τ of 8.15 would occur by chance less than once in one hundred thousand cases. We would summarise the relationship between the two ratings thus: $\tau = 0.835$, $\tau = 8.15$, $p < 0.00001$.

Partial Correlation

Partial correlation is a statistical device which permits us to consider the relationship between two variables while holding constant the effects of some third variable. At the beginning of this chapter we said that indices of correlation describe the extent to which variations in one item change along with variations on another. We also pointed to the aim of science to reduce the complexity of the phenomena being studied. Partial correlation is one of the simpler steps we can take in seeking parsimony. While it is possible to calculate partial correlations for rho and tau (τ) as well as for the product moment index, it is the latter which is usually involved.

Table 9.5 shows some hypothetical correlations between three assessments of competence in a class of social work students.

TABLE 9.5. CORRELATION BETWEEN THREE ASSESSMENT METHODS

	1	2	3
1. Assessment by field work tutor	—	0.45	0.51
2. Assessment by academic tutor	0.45	—	0.55
3. Class exam results	0.51	0.55	—
$(N = 40)$			

The reader can satisfy himself that all three correlations are statistically significant by applying the t-test formula:

$$t = \frac{r\sqrt{N-2}}{\sqrt{1-r^2}}; \text{ with d.f.} = N - 2.$$

The correlations in Table 9.5 indicate that the two tutors agree to a significant degree in their assessment of competence and that both agree with a student assessment based on the results of class examinations on a variety of social work subjects. If we think that there is some feature of competence in social work which is not adequately tapped by examinations but can be assessed by tutors, then we would expect that tutor assessments would still be positively correlated when we had taken account of the fact that both tutor assessments were positively related to exam results. Partial correlation is a technique whereby we can test this expectation; we can "partial out" or hold constant the variations in competence measured by exams and then see whether the two raters still show a relationship in how they assess their students. The formula for partial correlation is:

$$r_{12 \cdot 3} = \frac{r_{12} - (r_{13})(r_{23})}{\sqrt{1 - r_{13}^2}\,\sqrt{1 - r_{23}^2}},$$

where $r_{12 \cdot 3}$ is the product moment correlation between variables 1 and 2 when the effects of variable 3 are held constant, r_{12} is the correlation between variables 1 and 2, r_{13} the correlation between variables 1 and 2 and r_{23} is the correlation between variables 2 and 3. For the data in Table 9.5 we get:

$$r_{12 \cdot 3} = \frac{0.45 - (0.51)\,(0.55)}{\sqrt{1 - (0.51)^2}\,\sqrt{1 - (0.55)^2}}$$

$$= 0.24.$$

To test whether this correlation is statistically significant, we apply a t-test similar to the one used for the ordinary product–moment correlation. Our degrees of freedom in the partial correlation case are $N - 3$, so that the formula becomes:

$$t = \frac{r\sqrt{N - 3}}{\sqrt{1 - r}}, \text{ with d.f.} = N - 3.$$

For our partial correlation of 0.24 we find a t-value of 1.50 which is not statistically significant.

In considering the example used here, we would conclude that the two tutors agree on what they are rating largely because their assessments are correlated with the students exam performance. We could infer or interpret these results as showing that there was no social work competence which was being assessed by tutors but not by exams. The use of partial correlation has clarified the relationships between the three assessment procedures (the reader can check that $r_{13 \cdot 2}$ and $r_{23 \cdot 1}$ are statistically significant). If we were to choose from these three (hypothetical) assessment methods we would choose that based on class exam results, since these correlate significantly with the two tutor assessments, even when partialling has been carried out. Thus some parsimony has been achieved.

It is possible to extend the technique of partial correlation to more than three variables, but in practice this is seldom carried out. Partial correlation indicates the possibility of examining correlation coefficients in ways which will reduce the complexity of any set of data. Where there are many variables, the number of correlations increases very rapidly, *N variables will produce $\frac{1}{2}N\,(N - 1)$ coefficients.* If we have 5 variables in a study we produce 10 coefficients; if we increase the number of variables to 10, we then produce 45 coefficients, 15 variables generate 105 correlations and 20 variables, not a large number in social research, gives us 190 correlations. There are a number of statistical methods which can be used to "boil down" these large numbers of correlations to a smaller set of relationships which can be more readily comprehended. All of these methods depend on the fact that if two variables are correlated then change in one variable can be used to predict changes in the other. How well these predictions can be made will depend on how well correlated the variables happen to be. Look again at the correlations between our two tutors in Table 9.5. Before calculating the correlation between their assessments we would have transformed these assessments into standard scores so that both sets of assessments would have a mean of 0 and variance of 1. We can conceive of the variance of our rater's assessments as all that went into the assessment. The fieldwork tutor, in considering the students, might have considered their punctuality, how they related to clients, how they related to staff, their knowledge of casework, their enthusiasm, etc. The academic tutor might have considered how they related to staff, their knowledge of casework, their enthusiasm, their ability to express themselves in a fluent manner, their ability to count, etc. These sources of variance can be expressed

$$\sigma^2 = a^2 + b^2 + c^2 + \ldots$$

where σ^2 is variance and a^2, b^2, c^2, etc., are various components. The variance of the fieldwork tutor's assessments could be represented:

$$\sigma^2 = a^2 + b^2 + c^2 + d^2 + f^2 + e^2,$$

where a is "punctuality", b is "relating to clients" and so on with all the various factors which influenced the assessments. It is customary to reserve e^2 to denote error in the variance. An example of error variance would be if the tutor confused James Smith with John Smith, thinking of one while entering the rating against the name of the other.

Similarly, the variance of the academic tutor's assessment could be denoted by:

$$\sigma^2 = c^2 + d^2 + f^2 + g^2 + i^2 + \ldots + e^2,$$

where c is "relating to staff", d is "knowledge of casework" and so on with all the various factors which influenced this tutor's assessments.

If we compare these sets of variance components we find that they have c^2, d^2 and f^2 in common. Any index of agreement between the two sets of assessments will involve these common elements. We can represent the amount of the variance of the field work tutor's assessments which can be predicted or estimated from the assessments of the academic tutor by r^2, the square of the correlation between the two assessments. Based on $r = 0.45$ we find that 20.3% of the variance on the first tutor's assessments can be predicted from the assessments of the second tutor. Almost 80% of the variance of the fieldwork tutor's assessments is unrelated to the variance of the assessments made by the academic tutor.

The notion of partitioning the variance of a test, or item, or assessment is an important one to which we will return. For the present it suffices to note that the *square* of the correlation between two variables indicates how much of their variance is common and hence how much scores obtained on one can be predicted by scores on the other.

CHAPTER 10

Surface Relationships Between Variables— Typal Methods

In the previous chapter it was indicated that quite a small number of variables can generate an embarrassingly high number of correlations. When planning a piece of research where an examination of correlations is to be a major part of the analysis, it should always be remembered that N variables produce $\frac{1}{2}N(N-1)$ correlations. It is always very tempting to add more and more variables to the research schedule, forgetting that this adds to the complexity of the results. Various statistical methods exist which enable the researcher to reorganise the information contained in a matrix of correlations or other indices of association. Such a reorganisation should simplify and accentuate the patterns of association which exist in the data. It should be emphasised that when analysing matrices such as these the same method of correlation should be used throughout. This chapter is devoted to three methods which reorganise the information by working directly with the matrix of correlations. Since these methods tend to group variables into types or clusters we will refer to them as *typal methods of analysis*.

We have chosen three of a family of typal analytic methods developed by L. L. McQuitty. These methods vary in the amount of information they extract from a table of associations and in the results they obtain. All three methods can claim to be simple, both conceptually and operationally, to be valid reflections of the original data and to have a wide sphere of application. Although we will use examples where the indices of association are correlation coefficients, it is quite in order to use any other index. All the methods work on the basic principle that every member of a type is more like some other member of that type than any member of any other type. While all of McQuitty's techniques conform to this basic principle, they vary in how closely they define types. Some of the methods have very demanding criteria for a variable to be regarded as a member of a type, the least demanding method, *Elementary Linkage Analysis*, defines the linkage between two items as being the largest association which a variable has with any of the other variables being studied. Thus every variable is assigned to a group or cluster in terms of its highest correlation.

As an example of how Elementary Linkage Analysis works, consider Table 10.1. A number of social indices of a town have been compared according to electoral ward boundaries and the similarities between pairs of indices are represented by the correlations in the table. The analysis of this artificial data consists of five steps:

1. Underline the highest entry in each *column* of the matrix. (In the table these entries are in *italics*.)
2. Select the highest entry of the entire matrix; the two variables having this correlation constitute the first two variables of the first cluster.
3. Select all those variables which are most like the variables of the first cluster. Do this by reading along the *rows* of the variables which emerged in step 2 and select any underlined coefficients in these rows.
4. Select any variables which are most like the variables elicited in step 3. If any variables emerge, continue the selecting process until no further variables emerge.
5. Excluding all those variables which fall within the first cluster, repeat steps 2 to 4.

If we apply these steps to our example two clusters emerge (Fig. 10.1). Adolescent Psychiatric Referrals (1) and Adolescent Attempted Suicide (2) form the first pair; Suicide (6) joins the cluster because its greatest similarity is with Adolescent Attempted Suicide. Road Accidents (7) also joins the cluster, its greatest association being with Suicide.

Since no correlations are underlined in row 7 this cluster is complete. Juvenile Delinquency (3) and Overcrowding (4) have the highest remaining correlations and form the nucleus of cluster 2. Local Authority Housing (5) has its highest association with Juvenile Delinquency

TABLE 10.1. CORRELATIONS BETWEEN SOCIAL INDICES

		(1)	(2)	(3)	(4)	(5)	(6)	(7)
Adolescent Psychiatric Referrals	(1)	—	*0.77*	0.12	0.11	0.09	0.55	0.41
Adolescent Attempted Suicide	(2)	*0.77*	—	0.14	0.13	0.07	*0.60*	0.40
Juvenile Delinquency	(3)	0.12	0.14	—	*0.65*	*0.59*	0.10	0.17
Overcrowding	(4)	0.11	0.03	*0.65*	—	0.52	0.09	0.20
Local Authority Housing	(5)	0.09	0.07	0.59	0.52	—	0.12	0.21
Suicide	(6)	0.55	0.60	0.10	0.09	0.12	—	*0.45*
Road Accidents	(7)	0.41	0.40	0.17	0.20	0.21	0.45	—

and in joining cluster 2 completes the analysis. Elementary Linkage Analysis uses only a little of the information in a correlation matrix. It concentrates on the highest associations between variables. In cluster 1 we see that Road Accidents is two steps away from Adolescent Psychiatric Referrals and Adolescent Attempted Suicide, the original entries in the cluster. In this particular example Road Accidents has high associations with both Adolescent Psychiatric Referrals and Adolescent Attempted Suicide, but in data where clusters have rather long chains of association, where "e" relates to "d" which in turn relates to "c" which relates to "b" which forms a mutual pair with "a", it is useful to have some means of assessing how close any individual variable is to the type reflected in the cluster. The *typal relevance* of variables can be determined by considering all the correlations between the variables of a cluster; variables which have high correlations with many other variables in the cluster can be deemed more relevant to the

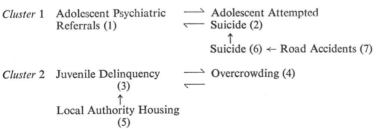

Cluster 1   Adolescent Psychiatric ⟶ Adolescent Attempted
                  Referrals (1)   ⟵ Suicide (2)
                                            ↑
                              Suicide (6) ← Road Accidents (7)

Cluster 2   Juvenile Delinquency ⟶ Overcrowding (4)
                      (3)   ⟵
                       ↑
              Local Authority Housing
                      (5)

FIG. 10.1. Clusters extracted by Elementary Linkage Analysis.

cluster than variables with lower correlations. Table 10.2 shows the two matrices of correlations for clusters 1 and 2 of our example. For most practical purposes it is sufficient to place the variables in rank order of typal relevance, we can do this by adding up each column of the cluster matrix and ranking the variables from highest total to lowest total. For cluster 1 our ranking is Adolescent Attempted Suicide, Adolescent Psychiatric Referrals, Suicide, Road Accidents; if we were to choose one index as being typical of those in cluster 1 we would choose Adolescent Attempted Suicide as having the greatest typal relevance. For cluster 2 the rank order is Juvenile Delinquency, Overcrowding, Local Authority Housing. Here we would consider Juvenile Delinquency as being the best representative of cluster 2. Typal relevancies are useful where clusters are so large that it is difficult to decide just how relevant some variables are to the cluster as a whole. They are also useful in situations where a matrix yields so many clusters that the available information is still quite complex. For example, if our social indices example had comprised 100 indices with, say, 10 clusters emerging, we could further simplify the results by grouping the clusters. This we would call a *second order* linkage analysis. To carry out such a second

TABLE 10.2. CALCULATING TYPAL RELEVANCE

Cluster 1	1	2	3	4
1. Adolescent Psychiatric Referrals	—	0.77	0.55	0.61
2. Adolescent Attempted Suicide	0.77	—	0.60	0.40
3. Suicide	0.55	0.60	—	0.45
4. Road Accidents	0.41	0.40	0.45	—
Sum of correlations	1.73	1.77	1.60	1.26
Rank order	2	1	3	4

Cluster 2	1	2	3	
1. Juvenile Delinquency	—	0.65	0.59	
2. Overcrowding	0.65	—	0.52	
3. Local Authority Housing	0.59	0.52	—	
Sum of correlations	1.24	1.17	1.11	
Rank order	1	2	3	

order analysis we would choose variables from each cluster which would represent their cluster at the second order level. For any cluster the variable with the highest typal relevance is the best choice to go forward to the next stage of analysis. Thus Adolescent Attempted Suicide would go forward to represent cluster 1 and Juvenile Delinquency would represent cluster 2. Quite often it happens that a cluster contains nothing other than a reciprocal pair, either of which could represent the cluster at the second order level. Accordingly, an alternative way of carrying out a second order analysis is to use the reciprocal pairs of each cluster. In either event, using reciprocal pairs or the variable with the highest typal relevance, a new matrix of correlations is formed and analysed as before.

Elementary Linkage Analysis provides a quick way of breaking a matrix of associations into a number of types which are fairly loosely defined. This loose definition is both the strength and the weakness of the procedure; it gives quick, comprehensive results, but at times produces clusters where variables have very little in common. If we wish to impose a more stringent criterion for membership of a cluster or type, we can use another of McQuitty's methods called *Typal Analysis.*

In this method a type is defined as a category of variables such that the members of the type are internally self-contained in being like one another. Every variable included in the type is more like each of the other variables in the type than it is like any variable not included in the type. The reciprocal pairs elicited by Elementary Linkage Analysis, Adolescent Psychiatric Referrals and Adolescent Attempted Suicide, Juvenile Delinquency and Overcrowding being the pairs in our example, form dyadic types. Adolescent Psychiatric Referrals in our example is most like Adolescent Attempted Suicide and *vice versa.* A triadic type can be identified when any three variables are identified as having their highest associations with each other; that is when each of the variables has its highest and next highest associations with the other two variables. Figure 10.2 shows two possible patterns of associations within triads. The figure indicates that for variables *P*, *Q* and *R*, *P* and *Q* form a reciprocal pair since each has its highest association with the other. Variable *R* has its highest association with *P* and its next highest with *Q*. For both *P* and *Q*, *R* is the variable with which they have their

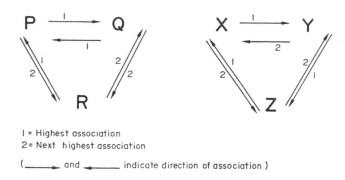

I = Highest association
2 = Next highest association

(⟶ and ⟵ indicate direction of association)

FIG. 10.2. Associations between three variables.

second highest association. Variables X, Y and Z form a triad without any two of them having previously formed a reciprocal pair. For a type of size N, every member of the type is more like the $N - 1$ other members than it is like any other variable in the data being considered. Each variable in a type will have its $N - 1$ highest associations with other variables in the type; in our triads the two highest associations of each variable were with other members of the triad, where the type has an N of four then each variable has its three highest associations with other members of the type, and so on.

The procedures involved in typal analysis are those of identifying dyadic types, adding variables to these types to form categories and then to see which categories re-emerge as types. Using our social indices example we rearrange the correlations of Table 10.1 in rank order from highest to lowest. We have found that the most practical method of carrying out this arrangement is to enter each correlation and its relevant variables on a slip of paper, arrange the slips in rank order and then to copy them onto the work sheet for the ensuing steps of the analysis. Figure 10.3 illustrates such a procedure while Table 10.3 shows the layout of the work sheet. In the table, reading from left to right, the columns present the correlation coefficients, their rank

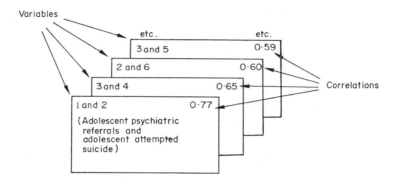

FIG. 10.3. Arranging correlations in rank order.

order, the pairs of variables having each association, the status of each step (whether the variables at that step are members of a type or a category) and the size of the type or category ($N - 1$). To the right of these columns are listed the variables being analysed.

We carry out the following steps on the work sheet:

Step 1. Enter the correlations, their rank order and appropriate pairs of variables in columns 1, 2 and 3.

Step 2. Select the two variables (Adolescent Psychiatric Referrals and Adolescent Attempted Suicide) with the highest correlation.

Step 3. Mark a 1 in the size column (col. 5); this shows that every variable in a category of two must be most like the one other variable on that category for the category to qualify as a type.

Step 4. Place a T_1 in column 4 to indicate that Adolescent Psychiatric Referrals and Adolescent Attempted Suicide form the first type.

Step 5. Proceed along the first row of the work sheet to the column headed Variable 1 (Adolescent Psychiatric Referrals). Place a 1-1 in the intersect. This shows that Adolescent Psychiatric Referrals is in T_1 and is most like one other variable in T_1. Similarly, proceed to the column headed Variable 2 (Adolescent Attempted Suicide) and place a 1-1 in the intersect. This shows that Adolescent Attempted Suicide is in T_1, and is most like one other variable in that type.

TABLE 10.3. WORKSHEET FOR TYPAL ANALYSIS

(1) Correlation coefficients	(2) Rank order	(3) Pairs of variables	(4) Type or category	(5) Size (N−1)	(6) Variables						
					1	2	3	4	5	6	7
0.77	1	Adolescent Psychiatric Referrals, Adolescent Attempted Suicide	T_1	1	1–1	1–1					
0.65	2	Juvenile Delinquency, Overcrowding	T_2	1						1–1	1–1
0.60	3	Adolescent Attempted Suicide, Suicide	C_1	2		1–2	2–1	2–1		1–2	1–2
0.55	4	Adolescent Psychiatric Referrals, Suicide	T_1	2	1–2						
0.50	5	Juvenile Delinquency, Local Authority Housing	C_2	2			2–2		2–1		
0.45	6	Overcrowding, Local Authority Housing	T_2^1	2				2–2	2–2		
0.43	7	Suicide, Road Accidents	C_1^1	3							
0.41	8	Adolescent Psychiatric Referrals, Road Accidents	C_1^1	3	1–3					1–3	1–3
0.40	9	Adolescent Attempted Suicide, Road Accidents	T_2^1	3		1–3	1,2–3				
0.29	10	Adolescent Psychiatric Referrals, Juvenile Delinquency	$C_{1,2}$	6	1,2–4						
0.26	11	Adolescent Psychiatric Referrals, Overcrowding	$C_{1,2}$	6	1,2–5			1,2–3			
etc.	etc.	etc.	etc.	etc.							

Step 6. Select the next highest correlation, this is between Juvenile Delinquency and Overcrowding. This also obtains a 1 in the size column (col. 5).

Step 7. Place a T_2 in column 4 to denote that Juvenile Delinquency and Overcrowding form a second type.

Step 8. Proceed along the second row of the work sheet to the column headed Variable 3 (Juvenile Delinquency) and place a 2-1 in the intersect. This shows that Juvenile Delinquency is in T_2 and is most like one other variable in T_2. Continue along the row to Variable 4 (Overcrowding). The 2-1 placed at that intersect shows that Overcrowding is in T_2 and is most like one other variable there.

Step 9. The next highest correlation is between Adolescent Attempted Suicide and Suicide. Adolescent Attempted Suicide is already in T_1 so the addition of Suicide changes T_1 into C_1 and increases the size of the category to 2.

Step 10. Proceeding along the third row to the column headed Adolescent Attempted Suicide we enter a 1-2, thus indicating that Adolescent Attempted Suicide is in C_1 and has its highest and next-to-highest associations with variables in C_1. Suicide is identified and a 1-1 inserted to show that it belongs to C_1 and has its highest relationship with a variable in C_1.

Step 11. The next highest correlation is between Adolescent Psychiatric Referrals and Suicide. This association changes C_1 back into a type which we label T_1^1. The size of the type remains at 2.

Step 12. At the intersects of this fourth row with Adolescent Psychiatric Referrals and Suicide we enter 1-2's to show that these variables are in T_1^1 and have their highest and next highest correlations with other members of that type.

The next two rows mark the addition of Local Authority Housing to Juvenile Delinquency and then Overcrowding, T_2 widening to C_2 and then regaining its status as a type, T_2^1. Rows 7 to 9 see the addition of the last index, Road Accidents, to T_1. In row 7, type T_1^1 expands to C_1^1, and by row 9 has re-emerged as a type, namely, T_1^2.

By row 9 all the variables have been allocated to a category or type so that all the remaining rows plot the steps towards one huge type encompassing all the variables. Accordingly we can terminate our analysis at row 9. It can be seen in rows 10 and 11 that both types T_1^2

and T_2^1 join to form category $C_{1,2}$ which has an $N - 1$ of 6, it encompasses all the variables.

The crucial aspect of Typal Analysis is in the distinction between *categories* and *types*. A variable enters a category by virtue of its highest correlation, just as in Elementary Linkage Analysis where a variable becomes a member of a cluster on the basis of its highest correlation. This means that in a category, as in a cluster, it is possible to find a variable which relates very highly with one other variable but not at all highly with other variables in that category. For a category to qualify as a type, each variable in the category must be more like each of the other variables in that category than it is like any other variable belonging to another category. If the reader looks again at Fig. 10.2 he will see that variables P and Q, a reciprocal pair, form a type. When we add variable R, which has its highest association with P, the type changes to a category since we cannot state for sure that R is more like P and Q than it is like any other variable in another category. Once we come to the step which links R and Q the category becomes a type once again since each of the three variables is more like the other two in the category than it is like any other variable not in the category.

From the work sheet we can abstract information about the typal structure of our example. Two dyads are first to appear, Adolescent Psychiatric Referrals and Adolescent Attempted Suicide in the first row, Juvenile Delinquency and Overcrowding in the second. By the fourth row Suicide has joined Adolescent Psychiatric Referrals and Adolescent Attempted Suicide to form a triad, the next row sees Local Authority Housing link with Juvenile Delinquency and Overcrowding to form another triad. By the ninth row Road Accidents has formed a tetrad with Adolescent Psychiatric Referrals, Adolescent Attempted Suicide and Suicide. Thus, this method of analysis yields two ultimate types in the group, one of four variables, the other of three. At various steps in the analysis we can determine whether types within these final types occur.

A very important feature of this method is that it can be used to test hypotheses about the existence of types in data. If the variables under scrutiny tend to form one large category without first yielding types then we can conclude that our data does not have a clear typal structure.

The third main method of clustering that we will set out is called

Hierarchical Syndrome Analysis. This method is particularly useful when we suspect that our data comprises variables which relate in a hierarchical manner. The classification of animals into species, genera and so on is the best known example of a hierarchical system where each level of the classification can be useful for specific purposes. Once again, the purpose of the method is to classify variables so that every variable in any category is more like every other variable in that category than it is like any other variable belonging to any other category.

Beginning once again with our matrix of correlations in Table 10.1, Hierarchical Syndrome Analysis proceeds with the following steps:

Step 1. Select the highest entry in the matrix. This is 0.77 and relates Adolescent Psychiatric Referrals with Adolescent Attempted Suicide. These two variables can be grouped into a category and this category can replace each of them in further analysis.

Step 2. Table 10.4 shows the succeeding matrices formed in the analysis. *Matrix a* lists the new category Apr, Aas, which replaces Adolescent Psychiatric Referrals and Adolescent Attempted Suicide. In determining which correlations Apr, Aas shall have with the other variables, we choose the lower of the possible pairs of correlations. For instance, Juvenile Delinquency correlated 0.12 with Adolescent Psychiatric Referrals and 0.14 with Adolescent Attempted Suicide so we take the lowest of these to represent our index of agreement between Juvenile Delinquency and Apr, Aas.

Step 3. We select the highest entry in our new matrix. This is 0.65 and relates Juvenile Delinquency to Overcrowding. These two indices can now be grouped into a category Jd, Ov, which replaces each of them.

Step 4. Matrix b lists the new category Jd, Ov in place of Juvenile Delinquency and Overcrowding. Once again in determining which correlations the new category shall have we choose the lower of the possible pairs of correlations.

Step 5. Again the highest entry is selected. This time it is 0.55 and links Suicide with our first category Apr, Aas. This creates a more inclusive category Apr, Aas, Su.

Step 6. Matrix c is created in a manner analogous to matrices a and b.

Step 7. Selection of the highest entry in the matrix links Local Authority Housing with our second category Jd, Ov thus forming a wider category Jd, Ov, Lah.

TABLE 10.4. MATRICES FORMED IN STEPS OF
HIERARCHICAL SYNDROME ANALYSIS

Matrix a	Apr, Aas	Jd	Ov	Lah	Su	Ra
Apr, Aas		0.12	0.03	0.07	0.55	0.40
Jd	0.12		*0.65*	0.59	0.10	0.17
Ov	0.03	*0.65*		0.52	0.09	0.20
Lah	0.07	0.59	0.52		0.12	0.21
Su	0.55	0.10	0.09	0.12		0.45
Ra	0.40	0.17	0.20	0.21	0.45	

Matrix b	Apr, Aas	Jd, Ov	Lah	Su	Ra
Apr, Aas		0.03	0.07	*0.55*	0.40
Jd, Ov	0.03		0.52	0.09	0.17
Lah	0.07	0.52		0.12	0.21
Su	*0.55*	0.09	0.12		0.45
Ra	0.40	0.17	0.21	0.45	

Matrix c	Apr, Aas, Su	Jd, Ov	Lah	Ra
Apr, Aas, Su		0.03	0.07	0.40
Jd, Ov	0.03		*0.52*	0.17
Lah	0.07	*0.52*		0.21
Ra	0.40	0.17	0.21	

Matrix d	Apr, Aas, Su	Jd, Ov, Lah	Ra
Apr, Aas, Su		0.03	*0.40*
Jd, Ov, Lah	0.03		0.17
Ra	*0.40*	0.17	

Matrix e	Apr, Aas, Su, Ra	Jd, Ov, Lah
Apr, Aas, Su, Ra		*0.03*
Jd, Ov, Lah	*0.03*	

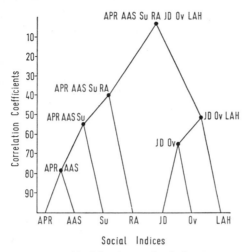

Fig. 10.4. Hierarchical Syndrome Analysis of social indices.

Two further cycles of forming a new matrix and selecting the highest correlation are necessary to complete the analysis. The first cycle relates Road Accidents to Apr, Aas, Su and the second cycle links Apr, Aas, Su, Ra with Jd, Ov, Lah.

Figure 10.4 shows how the categories relate from the individual variables up to the complete group. To avoid confusion the order of the variables is rearranged so that similar variables are placed together.

Applying Typal Methods to Empirical Data

The three kinds of typal methods dealt with in this chapter thus far have been presented using contrived data which produce clear-cut results. When these methods are applied to empirical data the results are not always so clear. Typal Analysis in particular seldom yields results which are as neat and tidy as our example. The definition of a type is highly demanding which makes the technique a powerful hypothesis-testing procedure. Elementary Linkage Analysis and Hierarchical Syndrome Analysis are less demanding than Typal Analysis, but even so some empirical data can produce strange results.

The new example is one involving real data from a study which aimed to elicit the conceptual framework used by a social worker to describe her clients. Preliminary enquiry showed that this social worker used fifteen descriptive terms to describe her clients and these terms, listed in Table 10.5, were applied by her to a consecutive series of clients. Each client was given a score on each descriptive concept and the relationship between each pair of concepts established using correlation coefficients. Table 10.6 shows the resulting matrix of correlations.

Elementary Linkage Analysis of the matrix appearing in Table 10.6 gives three clusters (Fig. 10.5). The first cluster tackles a problem not previously presented, how to deal with a *negative* correlation between two variables. Concept 7 has negative correlations with all the other concepts in cluster 1, and so has been phrased negatively. Cluster 2 shows a straightforward negative relationship between concepts 5 and 11, thus concept 5 is expressed negatively. In cluster 3 the reciprocal pair are negatively related. In this cluster concepts 1 and 14 are also negatively related to concept 12 resulting in the latter being expressed in a negative manner. Concept 13, having a negative relationship with concept 14, is also rephrased. Where negative correlations are present, great care should be taken to identify the best variables to rephrase.

TABLE 10.5. CLIENT DESCRIPTIONS USED BY A
SOCIAL WORKER

Concept

1. A client who is highly motivated
2. A client with whom I spend much time
3. A client I like
4. A pathetic client
5. A reasonable client
6. A co-operative client
7. A sensible client
8. A smelly client
9. An inadequate client
10. An insecure client
11. An unstable client
12. An aggressive client
13. An ineffective client
14. An emotionally motivated client
15. An approachable client

TABLE 10.6. CORRELATIONS BETWEEN CONCEPTS

Concept	1	2	3	4	5	6	7	8	9	10	11	12	13	14	15
1		0.032	0.154	-0.143	0.050	-0.082	-0.014	-0.111	0.161	-0.079	0.089	-0.443	-0.207	0.096	0.221
2	0.032		0.379	-0.018	-0.211	0.150	0.029	0.479	0.300	-0.071	-0.093	-0.421	-0.164	0.511	0.293
3	0.154	0.379		-0.175	0.396	0.439	0.232	0.039	-0.036	-0.446	-0.518	-0.564	-0.229	0.214	0.614
4	-0.143	-0.018	-0.175		-0.596	-0.371	-0.857	0.486	0.396	0.486	0.618	0.561	0.386	-0.271	-0.479
5	0.050	-0.211	0.396	-0.596		0.536	0.661	-0.432	-0.343	-0.739	-0.793	-0.357	-0.425	0.082	0.532
6	-0.082	0.150	0.439	-0.371	0.536		0.607	-0.354	-0.171	-0.679	-0.679	-0.443	-0.032	0.318	0.793
7	-0.014	0.029	0.232	-0.857	0.661	0.607		-0.064	-0.564	-0.721	-0.775	-0.607	-0.539	0.443	0.668
8	-0.111	0.479	0.039	0.486	-0.432	-0.354	-0.064		0.296	0.275	0.350	0.054	0.225	-0.032	-0.261
9	0.161	0.300	-0.036	0.396	-0.343	-0.171	-0.564	0.296		0.443	0.361	0.346	0.389	-0.107	-0.168
10	-0.079	-0.071	-0.446	0.486	-0.739	-0.679	-0.721	0.275	0.443		0.829	0.643	0.421	-0.346	-0.736
11	0.089	-0.093	-0.518	0.618	-0.793	-0.679	-0.775	0.350	0.361	0.829		0.829	0.457	-0.221	-0.718
12	-0.443	-0.421	-0.564	0.561	-0.357	-0.443	-0.607	0.054	0.346	0.643	0.529		0.432	-0.557	-0.818
13	-0.207	-0.164	-0.229	0.386	-0.425	-0.032	-0.539	0.225	0.389	0.421	0.457	0.432		-0.546	-0.264
14	0.096	0.511	0.214	-0.271	0.082	0.318	0.443	-0.032	-0.107	-0.346	-0.221	-0.557	-0.546		0.443
15	0.221	0.293	0.614	-0.479	0.532	0.793	0.668	-0.261	-0.168	-0.736	-0.718	-0.818	-0.264	0.443	

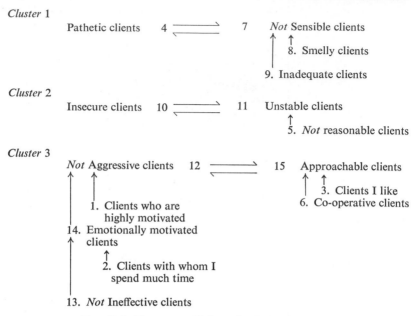

FIG. 10.5. Elementary Linkage Analysis of concepts.

In calculating typal relevancies on sub-matrices where negative correlations are present, it is necessary to carry out the procedure known as *reflection* before adding up the columns of the matrix. Consider matrix A of Table 10.7. In this matrix are entered the inter-correlations relevant to cluster 1, complete with minus signs where appropriate, taken from Table 10.6. It can be seen at a glance that all the minus signs are associated with concept 7. First we proceed along the row of concept 7's correlations changing each negative sign into a positive one (and had there been positives, changing them into negative). Then we go down each column of concept 7's correlations again changing the signs from negative to positive (and *vice versa* had there been positive signs).

Matrix B shows the results of this procedure. Concept 7 is prefixed by an "R" to indicate that its correlations have reflected signs, and since no negative signs remain we can add up the columns to determine the most relevant concept. For cluster 1 it is *concept 7*.

TABLE 10.7. REFLECTING THE SIGN OF CORRELATIONS IN A MATRIX

Matrix A Concepts	4	7	8	9
4		−0.857	0.486	0.396
7	−0.857		−0.604	−0.564
8	0.486	−0.604		0.296
9	0.396	−0.564	0.296	

Matrix B Concepts	4	7	8	9
4		+0.857	0.486	0.396
R 7	+0.857		+0.604	+0.564
8	0.486	+0.604		0.296
9	0.396	+0.564	0.296	

	4	7	8	9
Col. totals	1.739	2.025	1.386	1.256
Rank order	2	1	3	4

Reflection changes the algebraic sign of a correlation coefficient but does not otherwise affect the relationship expressed by the coefficient; it does not affect the *size* of the relationship. It is therefore a very useful procedure where we are concerned with looking at the *magnitude* of various relationships without being concerned about the *direction* of such relationships.

The reader should calculate the typal relevancies for clusters 2 and 3 using Table 10.7 as a guide. He should find that concept 11 best represents cluster 2, while concept 12 is the best representative of cluster 3. In reflecting the signs for cluster 3's correlation he will find that a small negative correlation (between concepts 1 and 6) remains after reflection. For the present purpose, that of calculating typal relevancies, this discrepancy can be ignored and the sign made positive. There are other statistical procedures involving reflection where this discrepancy would not be ignored.

How do we use Elementary Linkage Analysis to clarify our awareness of how this social worker views her clients? Cluster 1 shows that she sees pathetic, smelly or inadequate clients as not being sensible; we might wish to explore further what she means by "sensible". Cluster

2 groups together the concepts of insecurity, instability and unreasonableness as applied to clients. The high correlations between these concepts and the lack of variation in the size of the typal relevancies of this cluster indicate that these terms are interchangeable. Cluster 3 is large but clearly indicates relationships between liking clients and seeing them as approachable and co-operative; between seeing them as being motivated and spending much time with them. The relationship between seeing highly motivated patients as being those who are not aggressive has implications for predicting the professional behaviour of this social worker!

Following the Elementary Linkage Analysis of this data we might wish to ascertain whether the concepts grouped into types or close knit groups. Table 10.8 shows the worksheet for a Typal Analysis of the data. Apart from the three dyads or reciprocal pairs of concepts which were previously identified by Elementary Linkage Analysis, no types emerge. When we reach the coefficient which is eighth highest in rank order, column 4 indicates that all the earlier types and categories have merged into one. In practice the analysis can be terminated at this point, but if the reader continues he will have to carry on until he reaches the correlation with a rank of 43 before he can say that each concept has appeared at least once.

Interpretation of this Typal Analysis is easy. Apart from the reciprocal pairs already identified by the Elementary Linkage Analysis, the data does not fall into well-defined types of concept.

A Hierarchical Syndrome Analysis of this data produces the results shown in Fig. 10.6. When working with correlations it is possible to apply our ability to calculate the statistical significance of coefficients to make decisions about which parts of the hierarchical structure are important. Let us suppose that our social worker had rated 20 clients so that the correlations were based on $N = 20$. For this size of sample a coefficient is statistically significant at the 5% level of probability if it is greater than 0.44. If we draw a line on Fig. 10.6 at right angles to the vertical axis at the point representing 0.44 we can state that all the analysis below that line is based on significant correlations.

Such a decision would allow us to say that the social worker's concepts fall into four groups with three concepts left over. Concepts 4 and 7 are highly (negatively) related and are joined by concept 8 to

TABLE 10.8. WORKSHEET FOR A TYPAL ANALYSIS OF CONCEPTS

(1) Correlation coefficients	(2) Rank order	(3) Pairs of variables	(4) Type of category	(5) Size (N−1)	(6) Variables														
					1	2	3	4	5	6	7	8	9	10	11	12	13	14	15
−0.857	1	4, 7	T_1	1				1–1			1–1								
0.829	2	10, 11	T_2	1										2–1	2–1				
−0.818	3	12, 15	T_3	1												3–1			3–1
0.793	4	6, 15	C_3	2						3–1									3–2
−0.793	5	5, 11	C_2	2					2–1						2–2				
−0.775	6	7, 11	$C_{1,2}$	4							1,2–2				1,2–3				
−0.739	7	5, 10	$C_{1,2}$	4					1,2–2					1,2–2					
−0.736	8	10, 15	$C_{1,2,3}$	7										1,2,3–3					1,2,3–3
etc.	etc.	etc.	etc.	etc.															

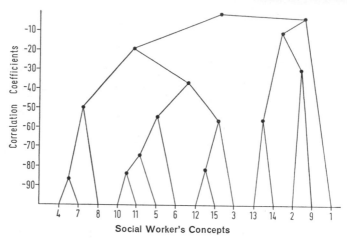

FIG. 10.6. Hierarchical Syndrome Analysis of concepts.

form the first group. Concepts 10 and 11 are joined first by concept 5 and then by concept 6 to form group 2. The third of our reciprocal pairs, concepts 12 and 15, form group 3 along with concept 3. Concepts 13 and 14 link up to form the fourth group.

In our contrived example of Hierarchical Linkage Analysis we stated (step 2) that when determining the correlations a combined category would have with other variables, the rule was to take the lower of the possible pairs of correlations. As a consequence of this rule it is possible to implement what McQuitty calls the *classification assumption*; that is, all members of a group or category at a particular level in the analysis can be assumed to have as many common characteristics as are possessed by the pair with the fewest. In our social worker example we were able to group together concepts 4, 7 and 8. Looking at the matrix of correlations in Table 10.6 we can see that the lowest relationship in the group is between concepts 4 and 8 ($r = 0.486$). This correlation gives us a conservative estimate of how much the concepts in the group have in common. The higher this conservative estimate is, the more similarity between the variables in the group.

References

McQUITTY, L. L. (1957) Elementary linkage analysis for isolating orthogonal and oblique types and typal relevancies. *Educ. Psychol. Measmt.* **17,** 207–229.
McQUITTY, L. L. (1961) Typal analysis. *Educ. Psychol. Measmt.* **21,** 677–696.
McQUITTY, L. L. (1966) Improved hierarchical syndrome analysis of discrete and continuous data. *Educ. Psychol. Measmt.* **26,** 577–582.

CHAPTER 11

Underlying Relationships
between Variables—Dimensional Methods

IN describing the technique of partial correlation in Chapter 9 we introduced the reader to the idea that part of the correlation between two variables could be accounted for by the associations which each had with some third variable. Remembering that a correlation coefficient is a means of expressing the way in which two entities vary together, we can say that it is an index of the *common variance* of these two entities. In our example of partial correlation (page 141) we indicated how our tutors made their assessments by considering different aspects of student behaviour. As part of the procedure of calculating the correlation between tutor assessments we would have transformed both sets of assessment scores into standard deviation scores so that both sets would have a mean score of 0 and variance of 1. The variance or variability of the assessment scores can be accounted for by students possessing varying amounts of the different aspects of behaviour being considered by each tutor. As in Chapter 9, the variance of the fieldwork tutor's assessments can be expressed:

$$\sigma^2 = a^2 + b^2 + c^2 + d^2 + f^2 + \ldots + e^2,$$

where *a* represents punctuality, *b* represents how students related to clients, *c* how they related to staff and so forth, *e* being reserved to identify error variance in the assessments. Punctuality, relating to clients, relating to staff and error are all sources of the variance in the fieldwork tutor's assessment. Such sources of variance can be considered as factors underlying the relationships between variables which we

165

usually express as correlations. If, in our example, the variance of the academic tutor's assessments can be expressed:

$$\sigma^2 = c^2 + d^2 + f^2 + g^2 + i^2 + \ldots + e^2,$$

where c is relating to staff, d represents knowledge of casework and so on, then we find on comparing the respective sources of variance that the two tutors have c^2, d^2 and f^2 in common. These three sources of variance determine the correlation between the tutors' assessments. We found, in Chapter 9, that only 20% of the variance of one tutor's assessments could be related to the variance of the assessments made by the other.

The results of our partial correlation exercise showed that when the results of performance on examinations were considered, the correlation between the two sets of tutor assessments dropped to a level which was not statistically significant. We could simplify the information presented in Table 9.5 by treating the variable "class exam results" as a factor underlying both tutors' assessments and thus considering the correlations which these assessments had with exam results as correlations with an important underlying factor. Figure 11.1 expresses in schematic form the path from individual assessment scores through correlations between assessment methods to a parsimonious result, namely, the correlation between tutor assessments and an important underlying factor or dimension. The figure summarises the mathematical procedures common to all dimensional methods which are used to identify the underlying relationships between variables. Using matrix algebra, these methods transform a correlation matrix, derived from the scores or values of persons or objects on a number of variables, into a set of dimensions on which the original persons or objects can be given scores or values. These new dimensions, usually fewer in number than the original variables, can be used to describe the persons or objects in a more parsimonious way. Put another way, these methods transform a matrix of correlations between variables into a matrix of correlations between the *variables and the factors* underlying the original correlations.

The dimensional methods set out in this chapter, principal components analysis and factor analysis, need access to a computer. The role of the computer in social work practice and research is dealt with

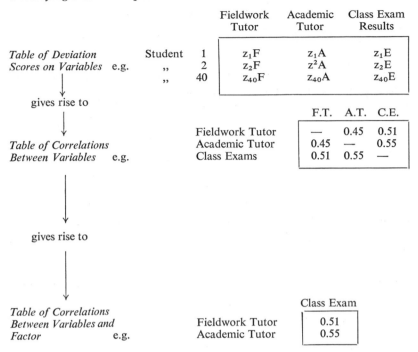

FIG. 11.1. Achieving parsimony in relationships between assessments.

in the next chapter. For the present it is sufficient to say that there are computer programs which will carry out the mechanics of analysing data in a speedy and accurate way so that these mathematically sophisticated techniques are at the disposal of a wide range of research workers whose interest is in the end product rather than the algebra. This situation has potential dangers, since for many researchers the choice of method of dimensional analysis may be arbitrary or may be governed by what is available at the local computer centre rather than by what is desirable in terms of the use to which the resulting data will be put. In consequence, our emphasis in this chapter is on understanding the purposes of the techniques and how to interpret the results of an analysis rather than to dwell on the algebra of the transformation process.

In common with the various kinds of cluster analysis techniques, factor analysis and principal components analysis aim to explain observed relationships among numerous variables in terms of a smaller set of relationships. Such a reduction in the complexity of any set of findings makes it easier for the human mind to grasp the nature of the relationships and to integrate this new information with existing knowledge and theory. This simplifying function is the way in which dimensional analysis is commonly used, but there are other ways in which the method can be applied. If we have identified a limited number of factors which explain the relationships between, for instance, assessments of students made by a number of social work tutors we could then go on to ascertain whether these same factors were present in assessments of students made by non-social work professionals such as general practitioners or clinical psychologists with whom the students had been working. Here dimensional analysis is being used as a hypothesis-testing method.

Whatever their function in any particular study, factor analysis and principal components analysis are *aids to thinking* about the relationships between variables. Before the advent of computer-aided data handling these methods of analysis were carried out only after a great deal of thought. Now, when the matrix algebra has been programmed and the computer can perform an analysis in seconds, it is tempting to factor analyse every correlation matrix in sight. Most researchers succumb to this temptation and painfully realise that sometimes factor analysis can complicate rather than simplify matters. It is very difficult to pass on this hard-won insight; each beginner has to learn it by himself. However, once factor analysis or principal components analysis are seen as aids to thinking rather than as a substitute for that activity, the way is clear to use these powerful methods.

Having indicated the value of the technique, we will introduce the reader to some of the special terms used in factor analysis. Consider the variance of some measure x:

$$\sigma_x^2 = a_x^2 + b_x^2 + c_x^2 + s_x^2 + \ldots + e_x^2.$$

The variance of x is made up of a number of *common factors*, that is factors which are common to a number of measures, labelled here a, b and c, a *specific factor*, s, which contains variance found only in measure

x and lastly an error factor, e, which identifies variance due to errors in measuring x.

If we applied measure x to a group of people on Monday morning and then applied it again to the same group on Monday afternoon we could calculate the correlation between the two sets of measurements in the usual way. This correlation would be an index of the *reliability* of measure x, an index of how consistent the measure was when applied on more than one occasion. In terms of the variance of x the reliability (r_{xx}) is all the variance except the error:

$$r_{xx} = \sigma_x^2 - e_x^2 = 1 - e_x^2.$$

The variance which can be attributed to common factors is called the communality (h^2) and can be expressed:

$$h_x^2 = a_x^2 + b_x^2 + c_x^2,$$

or it can be expressed as all the variance except that due to the error and specific factors, thus:

$$h_x^2 = \sigma_x^2 - s_x^2 - e_x^2 = 1 - s_x^2 - e_x^2.$$

The term "communality" will be used frequently in the rest of this chapter so the reader is advised to consider these formulae carefully.

Looking back to Table 10.1 our matrix of correlations between social variables, the reader will see that the diagonal running from top left to bottom right is blank. For factor extraction we need a complete matrix: if we are performing a principal components analysis we insert *unities* in each space along the diagonal, such unities representing the total variance of each variable in the matrix; if we are performing a factor analysis we insert *communalities* in each space. In terms of the formulae just spelled out it is readily apparent that in the principal components analysis, sometimes called the "closed model" of dimensional analysis, we have included various amounts of *specific* and *error* variance along with the common variance which we seek to resolve into factors. In the factor analysis, or "open model" of dimensional analysis, we have included only the variance which measures have in common. There are other important differences between these two models, but these are best discussed after presenting some worked examples of the two approaches.

Principal Components Analysis

Consider again Table 10.1 (page 145) in which are set out the correlations between a number of social indices. These correlations, which were contrived so as to provide good examples of typal analytic methods can be thought of as derived from a table of "scores" in which the frequency of occurrence of each index was recorded for each electoral ward of a town. The transformation of such a table into a table of correlations is taken a step further when we transform the correlation matrix into a table of correlations between our social indices and the factors underlying the correlations. These steps have been outlined in Fig. 11.1. This table of correlations between variables and factors is called the *factor matrix*. When we perform a principal components analysis, this matrix has a number of properties. The first is that the factor matrix will be as large as the correlation matrix; there will be as many factors as there are social indices. Secondly, the factors will be so arranged that the first will be the largest in terms of the amount of variance it accounts for, the second factor will be next largest and so on. Thirdly, the factor matrix when multiplied by its *transpose*, where each row of the factor matrix is written out as a column of the transpose matrix, reconstitute the correlation matrix exactly. This will be demonstrated as we work through the example.

We stated earlier that one of the main uses of factor analysis was to reduce the complexity of data. Taken alone, the transformation of a correlation matrix involving seven variables into a factor matrix involving seven factors fails to achieve such parsimony. However, since the factors are so arranged that the first of them accounts for as much of the variance as possible, with the second factor accounting for as much of the remainder as it can and so on, it is possible to discard the later, smaller components and attend only to the two or three which, in most cases, account for the bulk of the variance. In matrix terminology this smaller number of factors forms a *reduced factor matrix*. A reduced factor matrix multiplied by its transpose will yield an *approximation* to the original correlation matrix.

Table 11.1 shows the complete factor matrix of principal components derived from the correlation matrix in Table 10.1. The entries in the body of the table are given to five places after the decimal point, a

TABLE 11.1. COMPLETE FACTOR MATRIX FROM PRINCIPAL COMPONENTS ANALYSIS

Variables		Principal components						
		I	II	III	IV	V	VI	VII
Adolescent Psychiatric Referrals	(1)	0.75331	0.42221	−0.27361	0.14267	0.19704	0.19744	0.27144
Adolescent Attempted Suicide	(2)	0.75483	0.46432	−0.28518	0.02151	0.14210	−0.10745	−0.31799
Juvenile Delinquency	(3)	0.53267	−0.69372	−0.18368	0.08713	−0.01262	−0.42345	0.11926
Overcrowding	(4)	0.48779	−0.69931	−0.02968	0.34631	−0.24282	0.28407	−0.11202
Local Authority Housing	(5)	0.49246	−0.65564	0.04078	−0.48764	0.24368	0.16770	−0.02585
Suicide	(6)	0.71359	0.37899	0.07661	−0.29059	−0.50336	−0.02204	0.05458
Road Accidents	(7)	0.66372	0.13989	0.69667	0.16306	0.16297	−0.07338	−0.00138
Latent Roots		2.85474	1.95720	0.68368	0.49716	0.45745	0.34452	0.20522
Percentage of Variance		40.8%	28.0%	9.8%	7.1%	6.5%	4.9%	2.9%

degree of accuracy which is seldom required. This degree of accuracy will help when we reconstitute the correlation matrix by multiplying the factor matrix by its transpose. In most reports of factor analytic studies these *factor loadings* or entries in the factor matrix are given to the second or third place after the decimal point. The amount of variance accounted for by each component is found by summing the squares of each factor loading the component has with the variables in the study. For the first component this variance, found by $0.75831^2 +$ $0.75483^2 + 0.53267^2 + 0.48779^2 + 0.71359^2 + 0.66072^2$, amounts to 2.85474. This value is called the *latent root* or *eigenvalue* of the principal component with which it is associated. In the principal components model we have decided to include all the variance of each variable in the analysis, inserting unities along the diagonal of the correlation matrix. This means that the total amount of variance in any particular analysis will be the same as the number of variables, in our example there are seven variables so that the *total variance* is 7.00000. When we sum the latent roots of each component in Table 11.1 we obtain the value 6.99997. Allowing for small errors incurred by rounding off values during the analysis, we can see that the latent roots or eigenvalues add up to the total variance of the matrix. The total variance has been re-distributed so that the first two components account for over two-thirds of all the available variance. The last row of Table 11.1 indicates the percentages of variance accounted for by each component. These values are obtained by multiplying the appropriate latent root by 100 and dividing the product by the total variance.

The latent roots obtained for our example demonstrate very clearly that property of principal components analysis which allocates as much of the variance as possible to the first component, then as much of the remaining variance to the next component and so on. If the major aim of the analysis is to reduce the complexity of the variables under scrutiny then it would be acceptable to consider a reduced factor matrix, presenting the larger components only. In our example it is easy to decide that two components will suffice since they represent most of the variance, but it should be recognised that this is an arbitrary decision based on the great difference in the size of the latent roots of the second and third components.

It was indicated earlier that the correlation matrix could be reconstructed by multiplying the factor matrix by its transpose. Table 11.2 shows how this is done. The factor loadings of component 1 are set out

TABLE 11.2. RE-CREATING THE CORRELATION MATRIX

Loadings on component 1	Columns						
Rows	0.75831	0.75483	0.53267	0.48779	0.49246	0.71359	0.66072
0.75831	0.57503	0.57239	0.40392	0.36989	0.37343	0.54112	0.50103
0.75483	0.57239	0.56976	0.40207	0.64622	0.65241	0.53863	0.49893
0.53267	0.40392	0.40207	0.28373	0.25983	0.26231	0.38010	0.35194
0.48779	0.36989	0.64622	0.25983	0.23793	0.24021	0.34808	0.32229
0.49246	0.37343	0.65241	0.26231	0.24021	0.24251	0.35141	0.32537
0.71359	0.54112	0.53863	0.38010	0.34808	0.35141	0.50921	0.47148
0.66072	0.50103	0.49873	0.35194	0.32229	0.32537	0.47148	0.43655

as a row and column array around the margins of a matrix. The values in the matrix are obtained by cross-multiplying the marginal figures. The first value in the Rows margin is 0.75831; multiplied by itself (as the first value in the Columns margin) it yields a value of 0.57503; multiplied by 0.75483 it gives a value of 0.57239; multiplied by 0.53267 it gives 0.40392 and so on. When we repeat this cross-multiplication procedure for each of the six remaining components and for each cell of the matrix add all the values obtained we obtain the original matrix of correlations. Some of the values in some of the matrices will be negative and some will be positive; the reader should take careful note of algebraic signs when carrying out this procedure. If we had limited ourselves to the first two principal components, then our reconstructed correlation matrix would only approximate to the original matrix (Table 10.1).

Even in studies where all the principal components are extracted and presented, it is unusual for more than a few of the components, say a quarter of the total number, to be interpreted in any way. Table 11.1 shows that the first principal component in our example has fairly high loadings on all seven variables, the highest being Adolescent Psychiatric Referrals followed by Adolescent Attempted Suicide and Suicide. We might be tempted to label this component "General Social Malaise" or, if we ignored the fact that all seven variables have substantial loadings, we might call it "Adolescent Distress". The second principal component is *bipolar* in that it has negative as well as positive loadings. The largest loadings are for Overcrowding, Juvenile Delinquency and Local Authority Housing; these are at the opposite pole of the component from Adolescent Attempted Suicide, Adolescent Psychiatric Referrals and, to a lesser extent, Suicide. It is hard to find a label for this component. One solution is to concentrate on one pole only and call this a factor of "Environmental Stress". The reader might find it insightful to think of other suitable labels for these components. Most researchers try very hard to label the components which emerge from their analysis; if the reader has tried to produce suitable labels he should be aware that this task involves searching for a description which will "fit" the component. This search can extend well beyond the factor loadings, and can involve theoretical assumptions about how the variables "should" be related. The consumer of research reports should never take labels at their face value, but should always look at the pattern of factor loadings. Much of the time he will agree with the author's labels, but there are occasions where this will not be the case.

In cluster analysis it was possible to identify a variable which was typical of any one cluster. This possibility does not always arise when using one of the dimensional methods of analysis. In our example there is no ready conceptualisation for the pattern of loadings on the second component. When many variables are present it is useful to represent the loadings of variables on components in graphical form. This emphasises the *orthogonality*, or mutual independence, of the components and also shows up variables which lie close together in the charted space. Figure 11.2 shows how the variables in our example are related to one another in graphical terms. The clustering of Adolescent Psychiatric Referrals, Adolescent Attempted Suicide and Suicide on the one hand and Juvenile Delinquency, Overcrowding and Local Authority Housing on the other is at once apparent. It is clear that, whatever the mathematical advantages of the principal component model, the dimensions for our example bear little relationship to the clustering apparent on inspection of Fig. 11.2.

If the axis representing component 1 in Fig. 11.2 were rotated anti-clockwise until it passed through the point representing variable 2, Adolescent Attempted Suicide, and the axis for component 2 were

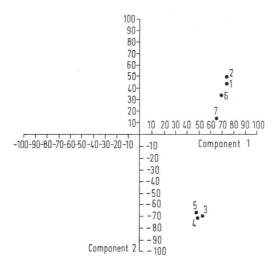

Fig. 11.2. Graphical representation of factor loadings on components 1 and 2.
Key 1, Adolescent Psychiatric Referral (APR); 2, Adolescent Attempted Suicide
(AAS); 3, Juvenile Delinquency (JD); 4, Overcrowding (Ov); 5, Local Authority
Housing (LAH); 6, Suicide (Su); 7, Road Accidents (RA).

rotated the same amount so that the new axes were still at right angles,
then such a *rotation* would bring together the dimensional and clustering conceptualisations of the relationships between the variables. This
procedure of rotation is a necessary part of the open model of factor
analysis, but its use in a principal components analysis must be questioned. The strong point of components analysis is that it presents a
mathematically unique solution in which each component extracts as
much variance as possible. This mathematically satisfying state of
affairs is achieved at the cost of including all the variance of each test
in the analysis, error and specific variance being mixed with common
variance. To rotate principal components is to destroy the mathematical properties of the solution while retaining the less desirable
property of having mixed common and error variance.

Factor Analysis

The 'open model' of dimensional analysis called factor analysis was evolved and developed by psychologists for psychological ends. The criteria which control the use of factor analysis are psychological-statistical rather than mathematical-statistical. In searching for a limited number of dimensions which can account for the relationships existing between a large number of variables, the factor analyst is concerned to find an "interesting" solution. Such a solution is one which helps to clarify thinking about some problem area and will facilitate the development of new ideas in the area. Factor analysis is not merely a statistical method, nor is it a routine which can be applied fruitfully to every correlation matrix in sight.

Factor analysis is concerned with the common variance present in a matrix of correlations. Variance due to specific factors and error is extraneous and uninteresting. The technique also aims to account for the many relationships between the original variables by as few factors as possible in a form which is "interesting" in the sense already described. These ends have led to a great deal of work to provide acceptable solutions to the three major problems posed by the open model. These problems are: first, how to reach the best estimate of the communality (h^2) of a variable; second, how many factors should be taken to account for the common variance in the date being studied; and third, how those factors should be *rotated* to a final solution which satisfies conceptual as well as statistical criteria.

The communality of a variable, as has been stated earlier, is all the variance due to common factors and can be written:

$$h^2 = 1 - s^2 - e^2,$$

where s^2 is specific variance and e^2 is error variance.

Since the reliability of a variable can be written:

$$r = 1 - e^2,$$

it is clear that the communality of a variable can never be greater than the reliability of that variable. Usually it is quite a bit smaller. The most acceptable initial estimate of the communalities to insert along the diagonal of the correlation matrix prior to the process of transformation is the *squared multiple correlation* which each variable has with the remaining $n - 1$ variables under study. The coefficient of multiple correlation indicates the strength of relationship between one variable and the others *taken together*. In the case of three variables this correlation can be expressed:

$$R_{1.23} = \sqrt{\frac{r_{12}^2 + r_{13}^2 - 2(r_{12}^2)(r_{13}^2)(r_{23}^2)}{1 - r_{23}^2}}$$

where $R_{1.23}$ is the multiple correlation between variable 1 and variables 2 and 3 taken together and r_{12}, r_{13} and r_{23} are the appropriately sub-scripted product moment correlations between the three variables. Mathematically it has been shown that the squared multiple correlation of a variable does not exceed the communality of that variable and most computer programs use squared multiple correlations as initial estimates of the communalities which can be improved by an iterative, recycling technique. It is not necessary for the reader to know how to do this, since it is built in to the computer program.

Just as there is no "Golden Rule" in finding the best estimate of the communalities needed in any particular case, so is there no cut and dried procedure for determining the number of factors which should be extracted in any given analysis. Many researchers extract quite a number of factors and then, quite arbitrarily, declare that only two or three are of interest. Usually this kind of decision is made on the basis of the percentage of variance accounted for by each factor and on the loadings which the variables have on the factors. Such *post hoc* decision-making is unsatisfactory but common, especially in Britain where, traditionally, factor analysts have preferred to extract relatively few factors from an analysis compared with American researchers.

As with the communality problem, there are mathematically based upper and lower limits to the number of common factors which can be postulated for any matrix of correlations. The upper limit to the number of such factors is a figure equal to half the number of variables being factored; in an analysis involving twenty variables we would certainly not extract more than ten factors. The lower limit for the number of factors is a figure equal to the number of latent roots greater than unity in the correlation matrix under examination. It should be noted that these are the latent roots found by applying the components analysis procedure to a correlation matrix having unities in the diagonal. This mathematically based lower limit has been found to be about just right for most factor analyses of psychological data and it is frequently incorporated in computer programs. For the most part this will be acceptable to the researcher, but there will be occasions when he will wish to look at a greater number of factors. If, in some analysis, the latent roots had values of 2.80, 2.00, 1.50, 1.03, 0.98, 0.53, 0.49 and so on, the "latent roots greater than one" rule would yield four factors as the best solution. The prudent researcher would note that the fifth latent root (0.98) was not much smaller than the fourth (1.03) and might decide to accept a five-factor solution as a reasonable alternative.

Having determined the communalities of the variables to be factored and the number of factors to be extracted, the factor analyst can proceed to transform a correlation matrix into a reduced factor matrix. Such a reduced factor matrix, when multiplied by its transpose, will give a reasonable approximation to the original correlation matrix. The reduced factor matrix can be transformed into an infinite number of other reduced factor matrices each of which would give the same approximation to the correlation matrix. Consider again Fig. 11.2 which expresses the loadings of variables on components 1 and 2 of our example in graphical terms. Variables 3, 4 and 5 form a triangle and it is at once apparent that the axes representing components 1 and 2 can be rotated through any specified degree without altering the relationship between variables 3, 4 and 5. The axes form convenient points of reference which allow us to plot out the relationships between the variables. Changes in the points or lines of reference will produce different coordinates for the variables, but will not change the spatial relationships between the variables. A homely example of the invariance of spatial relationships and the infinite number of reference axes is afforded by the annual event of decorating a Christmas tree. Imagine a large tree, in the middle of a room, hung with lights. The spatial relationship between any light and all the other lights is fixed; however, the view which a parent standing at the top of a step-ladder has is not the same as the view of a small child sitting on the floor. The same set of spatial relationships are described differently from the two viewpoints and, from the mathematical point of view, each description is valid. So with our reduced factor matrix, the factor loadings which can be used as coordinates in a geometrical representation give a valid representation of the original correlation matrix, but there are many other sets of loadings which are equally valid. The rotation problem is concerned to search for a particular set of factor loadings which will be mathematically acceptable and will also facilitate results which are "meaningful" in the context of the research study. In the past, rotation of factors on their axes had to be carried out graphically. Not only was this procedure laborious and time-consuming, but it led to criticism on the grounds that the results were "subjective". Most attempts at rotation are attempts to reduce the complexity of the factor structure of the variables being studied and the principles of *simple structure* enunciated by Thurstone (1947) underlie most rotated solutions. The criteria for simple structure are as follows:

1. Each row of the factor matrix should have at least one zero loading. (Where a *factor loading* is the correlation between a variable and a factor.)
2. If there are m factors in the matrix, then each column of the factor matrix should have at least m zero loadings.
3. For every pair of columns in the factor matrix there should be several variables whose loadings are close to zero in one column but not in the other.
4. For every pair of columns in the factor matrix a large proportion of the variables should have near-zero loadings in both columns, where there are more than three factors.
5. For every pair of columns in the factor matrix there should be only a small number of variables with non-zero loadings in both columns.

The ideal manifestation of simple structure would be where each variable had a high factor loading on one factor and near zero loadings on all the others, that is where nearly all of a variable's communality stemmed from one source. Such an ideal is seldom, if ever, achieved with empirical data, but it serves as a theoretical target, especially for the creation of mathematical computer programs which produce "objective" rotated solutions. The most frequently used rotation program is that using the Varimax criterion. The effect of applying the criterion to a column of factor loadings is to make large loadings larger and smaller loadings smaller. Due to its ready availability, and to its freedom from producing idiotic results, the Varimax criterion has come to be almost synonymous with simple structure.

The reader, especially if he is a consumer rather than producer of research, does not need to know much more about rotation. So far it has been assumed that rotation retains the orthogonality of factors, that is they remain independent and are at right angles to each other when plotted graphically. Orthogonal solutions are splendid when the main aim of the factor analysis is to reduce the complexity of the correlation matrix to a small number of dimensions which can be readily comprehended. If the aim of a study is to attempt to find factors which can be related to concepts and theories about some area, then it can be useful to allow the rotated factors to correlate with each other. Such solutions are called *oblique rotations*. In everyday life the dimensions of height and weight are conceptually independent although they are correlated; tall people tend to weigh more than short people. There are computer programs which give oblique rotated solutions, but their use is best left to experienced factor analysts.

It should be quite clear by now that there is a lot of thinking to be done before carrying out a factor analysis. A good computer program can make factor analysis easy, but the user should remember that the computer's solution has been determined by rigidly applied rules; the reader should now be aware of the fact that there are no absolute rules in many of the crucial aspects of factor analysis.

Our social variables example can be handled very adequately by a computer program. Inspection of Table 11.1 shows that there are two latent roots greater than unity and that there is a marked drop in size from the second to the third root; accordingly we will accept a two-factor solution. The correlation matrix, with squared multiple correlations inserted in the diagonal, is then transformed into a reduced factor matrix which appears as Table 11.3. The transformation procedure is the same as was used to find the principal components of the correlation matrix, so it is not surprising to find that the factors in Table 11.3 have loadings which are very similar to the loadings of the first two components in Table 11.1. The third column of figures in Table 11.3 shows the final communality of each variable. The reader can check

TABLE 11.3. INITIAL FACTORS FOR SOCIAL VARIABLES EXAMPLE

Variables		Initial reduced factor matrix		
		Factor I	Factor II	Communality (h^2)
Adolescent Psychiatric Referrals	(1)	0.74142	0.37975	0.69391
Adolescent Attempted Suicide	(2)	0.76238	0.43825	0.77328
Juvenile Delinquency	(3)	0.50537	−0.66570	0.69856
Overcrowding	(4)	0.43973	−0.63093	0.59143
Local Authority Housing	(5)	0.42503	−0.55266	0.48608
Suicide	(6)	0.63624	0.29504	0.49185
Road Accidents	(7)	0.53679	0.08453	0.29529
Latent roots		2.45328	1.57712	4.03040
Percentage of common variance		60.87%	39.13%	

that each figure in the third column is the sum of the squared values in the appropriate row of the other two columns, thus $0.69391 = (0.74142)^2 + (0.37975)^2$. As in the principal components solution, the latent roots for each column are obtained by summing the squared factor loadings for that column.

When the initial reduced factor matrix is rotated to meet the Varimax criterion of simple structure the result is the factor matrix appearing as Table 11.4. When Tables 11.3 and 11.4 are compared, it can be seen that while the communalities of the variables are unchanged, the pattern of factor loadings differs markedly. Factor I now has high loadings on four variables, Adolescent Attempted Suicide, Adolescent Psychiatric Referrals, Suicide and Road Accidents, with negligible loadings on the remaining three variables, Juvenile Delinquency, Overcrowding and Local Authority Housing. These three variables have high loadings on Factor II with the other four having small or negligible loadings. It could be argued that the loading of 0.19817 which Road Accidents has on Factor II is not negligible. To help in deciding when a loading is negligible we can use the formula set out by Harman (1967) which provides an estimate of the standard error of factor loadings in a

TABLE 11.4. VARIMAX FACTORS FOR SOCIAL VARIABLES EXAMPLE

Variables		Matrix rotated to meet the Varimax criterion		
		Factor I	Factor II	Communality (h^2)
Adolescent Psychiatric Referrals	(1)	0.83170	0.04673	0.69391
Adolescent Attempted Suicide	(2)	0.87934	0.00684	0.77328
Juvenile Delinquency	(3)	0.09993	0.82980	0.69855
Overcrowding	(4)	0.06083	0.76664	0.59144
Local Authority Housing	(5)	0.08768	0.69166	0.48608
Suicide	(6)	0.69814	0.06672	0.49185
Road Accidents	(7)	0.50598	0.19817	0.29529
Latent roots		2.22975	1.80065	4.03040
Percentage of common variance		55.32%	44.68%	

matrix. To be accepted as significant, a factor loading must depart from zero by an amount greater than the standard error figure given by the formula which is:

$$\sigma_f = \tfrac{1}{2} \sqrt{\frac{\left(\dfrac{3}{r} - 2 - 5r + 4r^2 \right)}{N}},$$

where σ_f is the standard error of the factor loading, r is the *average* correlation coefficient in the original correlation matrix and N is the size of the sample on which the correlations were obtained. The numerical values in the formula are constants.

Our correlation matrix was specially created as an example, not derived from the actual measurements on individual cases. For convenience, let it be assumed that $N = 23$. To find the value of the average correlation in the matrix let us use the formula established by Kaiser (1968) which states:

$$\text{Average correlation } (r) = \frac{\text{1st latent root} - 1}{\text{No. of variables} - 1},$$

where the 1st latent root is that from a principal components analysis *not* an analysis of the reduced matrix. For our example we get:

$$\text{Average correlation} = \frac{2.85474 - 1}{7 - 1} = 0.30912.$$

Inserting this value into the formula for the standard error we obtain:

$$\sigma_f = \tfrac{1}{2} \sqrt{\frac{\left[\left(\dfrac{3}{0.30912}\right) - 2 - 5\,(0.30912) + 4\,(0.30912^2)\right]}{23}}$$

$$= 0.26665.$$

For the data in this example it is possible to say that factor loadings of less than 0.26665 do not differ significantly from zero. Applying this to the factor loadings in Table 11.4 it can be seen that the Varimax rotation has yielded a very good solution in terms of simple structure. Each variable has a substantial loading on one factor and a negligible loading on the other. Two further points are worth noting. Firstly, the amount of common variance accounted for by each of the rotated factors differs from the percentage amounts accounted for by the unrotated factors. Second, the column of communalities indicates that the variable "Road Accidents" has relatively little in common with the other variables.

The rotated factor loadings produce a pattern of results which is similar to that produced by Elementary Linkage Analysis. While labelling of the factors must remain subject to the predilections of the researcher, this factor analytic solution is more parsimonious than the results of components analysis.

Dimensional Analysis using Empirical Data

As in the chapter on typal methods of analysis, we will end with an example involving real data. We have stressed that the results of principal components analysis and factor analysis should be related to the conceptual framework which generated the data being analysed. Only by doing this can these powerful statistical techniques be used to best advantage. When choosing between the mathematically satisfying technique of principal components and the conceptually oriented procedures involved in factor analysis, the researcher must base his choice on what he intends to do with the results. The example which follows deals with the conceptual and statistical properties of the five tests of hostility which comprise the Hostility and Direction of Hostility Questionnaire, or HDHQ (Caine, Foulds and Hope, 1967).

The origins of the HDHQ lie in the development of Foulds' theory of personality (Foulds, 1965) which lays stress on the need to consider the individual as a person in relation to others. The ability to enter into mutual personal relations with others is the hallmark of the mature individual, while egocentric thinking and behaving is characteristic of the immature. One feature of egocentricity is the need to apportion blame in any given situation, either to other people or to the self, so that hostility or punitiveness provides a useful operational measure of egocentricity. Three of the five tests in the HDHQ, Acting-out Hostility (AH), Criticism of Others (CO) and Delusional Hostility (DH), were designed to measure *extrapunitiveness* or hostility directed outward on to other people. The remaining tests, Self Criticism (SC) and Delusional Guilt (DG), were devised to measure *intropunitiveness* or hostility directed inward on to the self. These tests were conceived as measures of two different, but related, aspects of punitive attitudes.

Hope (1963) subjected the correlations between the tests to a principal components analysis and found a general component on which all five tests were positively represented, and a second components on which the extrapunitive tests were contrasted with those representing intropunitiveness. These two components, labelled General Hostility and Direction of Hostility, became accepted as best representing the variance of the five tests so that users of the HDHQ implicitly endorsed Hope's preference for principal components analysis rather than factor analysis in seeking to establish the underlying dimensions of a psychological test.

Table 11.5 presents a matrix of correlations between the five tests which make up the HDHQ. Based on the responses of 240 normals, it is at once apparent that all the tests correlate positively with each other. When this correlation matrix is transformed into the principal components solution, the factor matrix is as shown in Table 11.6. The first component has large positive factor loadings on all five sub-tests, while

TABLE 11.5. CORRELATIONS BETWEEN THE FIVE TESTS OF THE HDHQ

	AH	CO	DH	SC	DG
Acting-out Hostility (AH)		0.580	0.460	0.322	0.530
Criticism of Others (CO)	0.580		0.526	0.232	0.423
Delusional Hostility (DH)	0.460	0.526		0.250	0.467
Self Criticism (SC)	0.322	0.232	0.250		0.579
Delusional Guilt (DG)	0.530	0.423	0.467	0.579	

TABLE 11.6. PRINCIPAL COMPONENTS OF THE HDHQ

	Components				
	I	II	III	IV	V
Acting-out Hostility (AH)	0.757	−0.309	−0.438	0.280	−0.247
Criticism of Others (CO)	0.751	−0.440	−0.103	−0.447	0.179
Delusional Hostility (DH)	0.742	−0.277	0.529	0.274	0.133
Self Criticism (SC)	0.634	0.643	−0.224	0.106	0.351
Delusional Guilt (DG)	0.721	0.502	0.218	−0.204	−0.372
Latent roots	2.61	1.03	0.58	0.41	0.37
Percentage of variance	52.2%	20.6%	11.6%	8.2%	7.4%

the second component is bipolar. Self Criticism and Delusional Guilt having large, positive loadings while Criticism of Others, Acting-out Hostility and Delusional Hostility have negative, smaller loadings. These components are very similar to those obtained by Hope and taken together account for just under three-quarters of the variance. While we could happily follow the example of Hope and label these components "General Hostility" and "Direction of Hostility", we would find it more difficult to give names to the remaining components.

The components solution first produced by Hope and repeated here was never easy to relate to Foulds' original ideas, and following extensive use of the HDHQ with a variety of people, psychiatric patients, prisoners and many others, it was decided (Philip, 1969) that an alternative dimensional solution could be envisaged in which extrapunitiveness and intropunitiveness would constitute the major dimensions. Such a solution would be the result of a factor analysis where the initial factor matrix was rotated to satisfy the demands of simple structure. Because of the general inter-relatedness of the tests it was predicted that an oblique rather than an orthogonal rotation would best approximate simple structure.

Commencing with squared multiple correlations as the initial estimates of communalities and determining the number of factors by the "latent roots greater than unity" procedure, a factor analysis was carried out. Table 11.7 shows the reduced factor matrix and the final communality values while Table 11.8 shows the results obtained by orthogonal rotation to the Varimax criterion side-by-side with the results obtained by rotating to oblique simple structure. Harman's formula for calculating the standard error of a factor loading gives a value of 0.065. Applying this figure to Table 11.8, treating all values below 0.065 as zero, we find that in the Varimax solution all the factor loadings are

TABLE 11.7. REDUCED FACTOR MATRIX FOR THE HDHQ

	Factor I	Factor II	Communality (h^2)
Acting-out Hostility (AH)	0.668	−0.220	0.495
Criticism of Others (CO)	0.728	−0.413	0.701
Delusional Hostility (DH)	0.637	−0.157	0.430
Self Criticism (SC)	0.560	0.418	0.488
Delusional Guilt (DG)	0.696	0.452	0.689
Latent roots	2.180	0.623	
Percentage of common variance	77.8%	22.2%	

TABLE 11.8. ORTHOGONAL (VARIMAX) AND OBLIQUE ROTATED
FACTOR SOLUTIONS FOR THE HDHQ

Orthogonal Rotation			Oblique Rotation	
Factor I	Factor II	Variables	Factor I	Factor II
0.659	0.245	Acting-out Hostility (AH)	0.669	0.062
0.827	0.133	Criticism of Others (CO)	0.894	−0.119
0.595	0.275	Delusional Hostility (DH)	0.587	0.117
0.176	0.676	Self Criticism (SC)	−0.015	0.707
0.261	0.787	Delusional Guilt (DG)	0.046	0.804

significantly removed from zero. There is a fairly well-defined tendency for each of the five tests to have most of its communality explained by one of the two factors; Acting-out Hostility, Criticism of Others and Delusional Hostility have their highest loadings on Factor I, while Self Criticism and Delusional Guilt have their highest loadings on Factor II. The Varimax rotation has come closer to satisfying the principles of simple structure than the original factor matrix. Better still is the solution on the right of Table 11.8 which is the result of oblique rotation, the correlation between the factors being 0.525. Expressed graphically, applying the knowledge that the correlation between the two factors is the cosine of the angle between the axes representing the factors, Factor I lies at an angle of 58° to Factor II. Using the standard error value of 0.065, it can be seen that the loadings which Self Criticism and Delusional Guilt have on Factor I can be considered to be zeros, as can the loading of Acting-out Hostility on Factor II. The loadings which Criticism of Others and Delusional Hostility have on Factor II are non-zero but small. The oblique solution gives a good approximation to simple structure in which one factor accounts for the common variance of the three extrapunitive tests and the other accounts for the common variance of the intropunitive tests. This factorial solution has a clear affinity with the conceptual framework which generated the set of tests.

Inspection of the communalities in Table 11.7 shows that on average just over half of the total variance of each test can be attributed to common factors. The total communality in Table 11.7 equals 2.803, which when divided by the total variance of 5.000 equals 56.06%. This indicates very clearly that the components solution to the analysis of this HDHQ data contains a large amount of error and specific variance which is inextricably mixed up with the common variance.

This empirical example has shown how the two methods of dimensional analysis have been used to explore the structure of a psychological questionnaire. Had the HDHQ been created in a theoretical vacuum, then the principal components analysis of the tests might have been acceptable. But since the inventory was created in the context of a specific theory, any dimensional analysis has to satisfy conceptual as well as statistical criteria. Factor analysis allows both criteria to be applied and in this instance proves to be the more useful method.

References

CAINE, T. M., FOULDS, G. A., and HOPE, K. (1967) *Manual of the Hostility and Direction of Hostility Questionnaire* (HDHQ). London: University of London Press.

FOULDS, G. A. (1965) *Personality and Personal Illness*. London: Tavistock.

HARMAN, H. H. (1967) *Modern Factor Analysis*. Chicago: University of Chicago Press.

KAISER, H. F. (1968) A measure of the average intercorrelation. *Educ. Psychol. Measur.* **28**, 245–247.

PHILIP, A. E. (1969) The development and use of the Hostility and Direction of Hostility Questionnaire. *J. Psychosom. Res.* **13**, 283–287.

THURSTONE, L. L. (1947) *Multiple-Factor Analysis*. Chicago: University of Chicago Press.

CHAPTER 12

The Continuing Process of Research

IN the preceding chapters we have introduced the reader to the processes which underly the approach to conducting research and hopefully we have given sufficient guidance in the use of elementary statistics to enable the beginner to be able to choose the most appropriate techniques for his work. We have tried also to show how the research process and statistical methods of analysis become integrated in order to evaluate the data collected. We have emphasised that statistics are essential for the ordering of data from which meaningful inferences can be drawn so that informed decisions can be made. Given the necessary data which permit informed decision-making, it is important to realise that the researcher still has to *make* decisions and that these may still include value judgements. However, the use of appropriate statistics can help us to choose when a number of possible courses of action are open to us.

For example, if in a study using our Example 3 hypothesis which stated *There will be no difference between professionally trained social workers and untrained social workers in their attitudes towards the problems presented by clients*, it was found that there were statistically significant differences between the two groups in relation to "marital problems" and we also found that such problems tended to present on a particular day of the week, we would be in possession of information which could help us in decision-making.

If part of the aim of the study was to provide information which would assist in the deployment of staff, then these findings could help us to make decisions. Given that the marital problems came to the agency predominantly on a Monday and that the professional social workers were more positively disposed to problems of this type, then it would be a reasonable decision to ensure that a professionally trained worker would be on duty on that day rather than an untrained worker. One, of course, could not be certain that all marital problems would come on a Monday and that no other type would present, but from the research findings there would be a high probability that such worker deployment would be justified. The research findings only provide guidelines to decision-making, but other factors such as staff shortages and the personalities of the workers could influence the ultimate decision.

Any decision-making involves looking at a situation in the light of the information available at a particular point in time. Some of this knowledge can be derived from the quantification of available data and is therefore objective, but, on the other hand, some of the knowledge may be merely experiential. It is hoped that the reader will have recognised that there is a need in the research process for objectivity and a rigorous approach to the subject under study. Research is not just a matter of quantifying data. It is necessary to develop a critical approach which can help to sharpen practice. That is, it can help the practitioner to become more deliberate in his selection of treatment methods and techniques and to record client transactions in such a way that treatment can be monitored and therefore assessed.

Although much of this book is concerned with statistics, it is not the authors' intention to convert the social worker into becoming a statistician, but rather to enable him to be able to consume the product of research in a knowledgeable and critical manner and to conduct and plan research at a modest level. When embarking on a project, the social worker would be well advised to seek the expert help of a statistician and, where appropriate, a computer programmer. While the social work researcher need not possess all the statistical skills, he must know how to formulate the problems to be researched, since in the area of social work practice *he* is the expert and he is also accountable for decisions taken which affect the client. It is the aim of this book that the social worker should at least know what the various statistical techniques do and be able to judge their appropriateness.

Although statistical procedures are used after the data has been collected, they must be planned for in the design stage. It is no use collecting data and then asking the statistician or computer programmer what to do with it to make sense; sense only comes with prior planning and statistical techniques will not compensate for bad planning. The research process is not planned in isolation from data analysis. It is advisable to approach the data processing experts at an early stage in the study.

The use of statistics and of computers to analyse data have long been resisted by the social work profession on irrational grounds. Properly used, these tools help the professional worker to assess and improve the quality of his work.

What is a Computer?

The term "computer" does not refer to a single item of data processing equipment, but to the whole set of apparatus that is concerned with the manipulation and computation of data. Basically we can say that a "general purpose" computer consists of a central processor, input and output equipment, and a console—this is known as the "hardware". The major components of the central processor are the memory unit, in which information is stored either for use during a calculation or as data which is supplied for the machine before calculation commences; the arithmetic unit in which the information is processed; and the control unit, which directs the sequence of operations within the machine.

The input unit feeds information into the machine as well as coding the information into a form the machine can assimilate. At the other end of the process the output unit converts the material from the machine into recognisable form for our use, as well as printing out the information. These units vary from machine to machine and they may use different material, paper tape, magnetic tape or punched cards, as a medium for transferring the information into the machine. The console is the operator's link with the computer and it provides a visual indication of the status of the entire system and permits manual intervention in the operation of the system during the computing operation.

In computing, the term "program" (usually spelled in the American manner) refers to a set of instructions which are followed slavishly by the machine, and hence must be completely free from error, both from the point of view of the logic in which the problem is presented and the syntax of the particular programming language chosen. Programming languages vary according to the type of machine and the particular task to which the machine is applied.

The first step in programming is always an analytical definition of the bounds of the problem, followed by a breakdown of the problem into smaller workable units. With respect to the former, the particular problem to be solved is all too often formulated without being really understood and so lacks precision. One must decide what the program is expected to evaluate and what connections exist between the problem and other variables. Finally, there must be a high degree of accuracy both numerically and from the point of view of applicability. Once all these important questions have been asked we can then proceed to the analysis. It has been said that we may *think* that we know something when we first learn it, but become convinced that we know it when we can teach it. In fact we only really *know* it when we can code it for a computer.

Although the computer will undertake much of the tedious and complicated work, in any situation there is still the task of preparing the material, preparing programs and interpreting the results which the machine produces. This does not mean a reduction in the need for the human element in the computer world, but it means release for the human factor from much of what is at present non-creative work, and allows more time for creative expression.

The Use of the Computer

On first examination the idea of using computers in the social services may seem to be the antithesis of the main principles behind the services; individual, personally directed services, given by professionals working through an individually developed relationship with a client. The computer, on the other hand, is an impersonal means of achieving satisfactory completion of a task by removing sources of failure inherent in a human agent, speeding up of the process of task completion, and extending the range of tasks undertaken to include problems which had previously been outside the scope of the human mind. This impression may be given further weight because the computer is seen as a threat to the human element underlying the social services by being the main vehicle through which problems are solved.

Many people, social workers in particular, see the computer as a threat to their work; a non-human element moving into an area of work in which the human element is of prime consideration. This assumption is misplaced on two counts. Firstly, the computer is most frequently used in the cognitive field of functioning, whereas the social worker's skills are essentially centred in the emotive sphere. Although the social worker draws upon cognitive abilities in his work, the computer does not draw upon emotive qualities. Secondly the computer is not an autonomous unit, but is regulated in the tasks it undertakes and the directions it takes in solving these by human forces—the programmers and operators.

There is often a failure to understand the computer, for it is seen as a rival to the human mind, and not as it really is, its product. It is not a means of supplanting the workers in the social services, but of complementing their efforts and helping to extend the knowledge and skills in the human field. Many technological changes have done this already, for example the telephone, the typewriter and the dictaphone, and the computer is no different in its helpfulness.

Computers are already at work in the social services. Many large local authorities employ the resources of computers for wage and tax calculations, stock recording, machine control and basic data about clients. They have also been used to calculate payments made to foster parents, and to assess and record charges to be made on parents who have children in the care of the local authority.

It is not suggested that each social work agency or office should have its own computer, as the cost of this would not be feasible, in terms of capital expenditure or the time the computer would be used. But the position has now been reached that social services have direct access to a computer usually situated at the County Administrative Centre and used by a number of departments. Eventually area offices could have indirect access by direct "on line" equipment, that is a telephone link to a "slave" computer which could be used as a store, the main computer being supplied by the "slave" which would also be able to undertake small standard computational tasks. Use of time on the main computer could be allocated for specific large tasks, and its time rationed between several users.

Computer resources can be employed in the following ways:

1. ROUTINE TASKS

These are essentially repetitive tasks in which a large amount of data, with many variables, can be manipulated. The computer can act as a data analyser and store of information, rebalancing the store as new material is received. It is a means by which large administrative units can be made aware of day-to-day changes occurring in their areas. Details of new cases and completed ones can be tabulated from the records of each area office and sent under one set of instructions or "program" through the computer with the same program being used by each office over and over again. Some of the variables which can be accounted for by the machine are, for example, clients' coded identity, age, sex, religion, type of worker dealing with case, the type of help given, charges and allowances made, etc.

The information given daily by each office can then either be totalled cumulatively for the whole county, under any of the foregoing headings, or separately for each area office. Such information allows for an up-to-date picture of the social work scene and possibly facilitates regional planning.

2. RESEARCH

There are now available a large number of statistical programs which enable computers to be used for treating quantified data by statistical methods—examining data to see if a statistical relationship appears between any variables under study. The research social worker must be sufficiently versed in statistics to be able to select the appropriate program for each task he has in mind.

3. INVESTIGATION TASKS

These involve the analysis and separation of objective data from non-objective data in social relationship situations and thereby help to clarify possible areas for research.

Within the field of the social services there are identifiable common principles which underlie social work methods and techniques. As we have indicated, a social worker or administrator when arriving at a decision to do something does so on the basis of available data, his interpretation of it and a reliance on a particular skill or "feeling". The whole process of interpretation of data may be dependent upon training and observation of the work of other people, as well as upon personal experience from similar situations. It is important, however, to be able to know when skill is based on rational decisions and training and when it is no more than a personal feeling or a hunch. If it were possible to analyse the objective factors which are commonly assessed by a group of people in arriving at a particular decision, this would identify more clearly the area in which subjective elements play a part and possibly enable a clearer identification of the collective intuitive skills as opposed to personal "hunches".

Possible examples of this which are suitable for treatment by computer means would be to analyse the factors which were taken into account by a probation officer recommending probation in a report to a Court, a social worker recommending reception into care for a child or assessing whether or not a client is in need of residential care.

A possible approach in the first example would be to take a number of reports from a carefully selected sample of probation officers, all of whom had recommended one of the two possible ways of dealing with a case: (a) recommended probation, (b) not recommended probation, and then to tabulate the variables contained in their reports. It would then be possible to feed this data into a computer, by giving it a logical outline of the common factors which made up the decisions and to program it to make a decision on cases about which no human decision had been reached by using the findings from the other two sets of data. The decision reached by the computer could be matched against that reached independently by individual officers. Resultant differences in these decisions could, for example, point to the presence of possible unlisted variables (e.g. feelings) which would form the basis for exploration as to possible specialist personal skills which could then be identified and lead to a widening of existing social work techniques.

4. OPTIMISATION

The allocation of resources, particularly in the social services, is difficult because of the problem of measuring variables such as the "work load" of an individual when a non-tangible criterion such as casework success is used. However, as a start to the process of defining and measuring this, it may be possible to approach it indirectly by experiments in the optimisation of other more tangible resources, the cost of building one type of residential accommodation as opposed to another, or trying to assess the optimum level of working for a social worker. This latter could be tried by recording the variety of tasks and quantity of work measured in relation to a number of cases, time taken by various undertakings, travelling, dictation, discussions and the like in two area offices, as well as the costs involved; wages, rents, stationery, travelling expenses and other outgoings. By optimisation techniques it would then be possible to simulate the conditions of both situations for the computer to determine the optimum level of working from the material given. This would not give one solution to a situation, but it would give a series of conditions, with a finite set optimising one or other of the variables. Nor would it necessarily be the ideal state of functioning, but it would give an opportunity to examine existing conditions against the optimum level to see what problems, or difference in conditions between the two areas, prevented the optimum level from being achieved.

These examples given are, by necessity, only general ideas of the ways in which computers can be used in the social services. Much would depend upon the type of equipment used and the sophistication of the program language and the people creating the programs. One of the prime preparatory factors needing consideration would be the recording of data and efforts to quantify the data. This would require a situation in which records in the social service agencies were both realistic in terms of their utility, and were amenable to being processed for computer treatment.

However, despite the growth of computer facilities in local authority and university settings, not all of them are well endowed with facilities for statistics which are appropriate for research in the social work field. Because of this, the social worker must, as we have indicated, have sufficient knowledge of the required techniques with the knowledge he may then guide the programmer by telling him the type of program required to enable the findings to be related to the problem under investigation so that professionally appropriate decisions can be made.

We would emphasise that statistical and computing techniques, though sometimes complicated, are useful tools in research. The novice researcher is often dismayed by a feeling that before statistical procedures can be used they must be understood in basic algebraic terms. This is a false conception. The beginner need only know the function of statistical techniques and when to use them in much the same way as he knows how to use a car. To know how to use a car does not entail understanding the workings of the internal combustion engine but only to know how to change gears and stop when necessary. However, just as changes in car design enforce changes in their handling by drivers, so also do changes in statistical procedures bring about the need for new approaches. The researcher must keep abreast of such changes by reading and discussion in order to avail himself of any new and improved techniques.

Data Presentation

The main function of research is to create and expand a knowledge base. Social work, being very much in its infancy, still draws heavily from associated disciplines, but with growing research will also develop its own knowledge base. However, this can only be achieved if the product of research is disseminated to its practitioners in an easily consumable manner. We have concentrated on the need to approach research in a rigorous, objective manner and to use the most appropriate statistical techniques for the drawing of meaningful inferences. The reader of the resultant report must be able to follow and understand its contents, but may not have acquired the skills of the researcher. Because of this the researcher must know how to communicate his findings in the simplest possible manner and in such a way that both the sophisticated and the unsophisticated reader will derive the maximum benefit.

As an example of how data should be presented let us use a bivariate table of results from a study based on our hypothesis 3 (page 29). In examining the action taken by social workers on a particular group of clients according to the day of the week on which the client first presented at the agency, the following table was drawn up to display the findings (Table 12.1).

TABLE 12.1. ACTION TAKEN BY SOCIAL WORKERS ACCORDING TO THE
DAY OF THE WEEK (PERCENTAGES)

Action taken	Day of the week				
	Monday ($n = 66$)	Tuesday ($n = 61$)	Wednesday ($n = 36$)	Thursday ($n = 90$)	Friday ($n = 123$)
Referred to other agency	40.9	36.1	25.0	65.6	53.7
Further social work undertaken	24.2	32.8	33.3	8.9	8.1
Advice given	19.7	21.3	25.0	14.4	18.7
Money or material aid given	15.2	9.8	16.7	11.1	19.5
Total	100.00	100.00	100.00	100.00	100.00

$\chi^2 = 52.76$; d.f. $= 12$; $p < 0.001$ (based on raw scores, not the percentages).

POINTS OF NOTE

(i) The title of the table identifies both variables being examined.

(ii) The data is shown as percentages, so that comparisons between action and days can be made more readily than would have been the case had raw numbers been used, there being a different number of referrals for each day. The reader will notice that the word percentages is also given in the title.

(iii) The categories in each variable are clearly labelled.

(iv) The direction of the percentage scores is indicated by the position of the total (100.00).

(v) For the sophisticated reader the raw number on which the percentages are based are shown for each day without detracting from the clarity of the overall presentation. This enables the percentages to be re-converted into raw scores and therefore make it possible for the Chi-square value to be tested for accuracy.

(vi) The results of the statistical testing and the method used are shown immediately below the table in this case the Chi-square value ($\chi^2 = 52.76$) followed by the degrees of freedom allowed (d.f. $= 12$) and finally the statistical probability (p) of the Chi-square value in relation to chance ($p < 0.001$).

Thus the results are presented clearly and with sufficient information for the sophisticated reader to draw his own inferences, but the unsophisticated reader may not be able to take the fullest value from the information given nor will he understand the Chi-square information, degrees of freedom or p value.

It therefore becomes necessary to present the data from the table in simple, plain language so that he can know what the figures are all about. By doing this the sophisticated reader will also be able to judge whether or not the researcher has drawn the proper conclusions from the data. At this stage of data presentation the researcher is only attempting to provide clarity about the findings shown in the table and not to offer explanations for them. This is known as "interpretation" as distinct from "discussion". Returning to Table 12.1, the "interpretation" given immediately under the table would probably take the following form.

"It can be seen from this Table that referral to other agencies was the most common action taken by the social workers on every day of the week except Wednesday and was particularly high at the end of the week. Conversely the amount of further social work undertaken was lowest on Thursdays and Fridays but constituted the greatest proportion of disposal on Wednesdays. Generally the giving of money was the action least often used but was at its highest on Fridays. These findings are highly statistically significant and could have occurred by chance fewer than once in every thousand occasions. . . ."

One of the reasons for giving sufficient data in the table is to allow percentages to be reconverted into raw numbers. As we have indicated, this allows the Chi-square value to be tested by the reader, but the working table for this analysis can also be used to explain the findings shown in the table at greater depth. Although the analysis work tables are never presented in a report, we will present the one related to Table 12.1 in order to demonstrate its use.

TABLE 12.2. THE CHI-SQUARE WORK TABLE

Action taken	Day of the week					Total
	Monday	Tuesday	Wednesday	Thursday	Friday	
Referred to other agency	fe = 32.1	29.7	17.5	43.8	59.9	183
	27	22	9	59	66	
	$\chi^2 =$ 0.8	2.0	4.1	5.3	0.6	
Further social work undertaken	fe = 11.6	10.7	6.3	15.8	32.1	66
	16	20	12	8	10	
	$\chi^2 =$ 1.7	8.1	5.2	3.8	15.2	
Advice given	fe = 11.9	11.0	6.5	16.3	22.2	68
	13	13	9	13	23	
	$\chi^2 =$ 0.1	0.4	1.0	0.7	0.03	
Money/ material aid	fe = 10.4	9.6	5.6	14.1	19.3	59
	10	6	6	10	24	
	$\chi^2 =$ 0.02	1.3	0.03	1.2	1.1	
Total	66	61	36	90	123	376

$\chi^2 = 52.76$; d.f. $= 12$; $p < 0.001$.

It can be seen from our work table that the greatest contribution to the very high Chi-square value was the cell concerning further social work undertaken on Fridays. The next highest was further social work undertaken on Tuesdays, followed by referral to other agencies on Thursdays. These three cells accounted for more than half of the total Chi-square value and therefore further "interpretation" under Table 12.1 is called for and might continue thus:

> "... An inspection of the Chi-square table showed that for further social work undertaken on Fridays only one third of number of cases were observed than could have been expected had chance alone been operating while on Tuesdays the observed number of clients was almost double the chance expected frequency. On Thursdays it was noted that there were almost a third more than the chance expected number of clients who were sent to other social work agencies."

This added information has highlighted the need to draw particular attention to these facts later in the report.

We have drawn the reader's attention to the need to provide clarity in the presentation of data by concentrating on a single table of results. However, this clarity is basic to the entire research process and imperative at the report writing stage which is dealt with in the following chapter.

CHAPTER 13

The Research Report

THE report which arises from a research project can take many forms. It can be published as a book, a report to a sponsor or committee, as an academic thesis or as a paper for publication. Although each of these media of communication may require different presentation, common to them all is the need for the researcher to consider carefully the purpose of the report and the audience for whom the report is intended.

Given the obvious differences between these varieties of report, there are rules of presentation which apply to them all. Specific rules about presentation can be established by consulting the editor or academic board to establish the form a report needs to take and this should be done *before* the "write-up" is started. One important reason for this is to establish the length of the report. This will help to determine the relative weight which should be given to each section and will also ensure that the "house" rules are followed.

Rules of Presentation

1. All good written material should be clear, precise and concise and research reports must follow these elementary principles.

2. The title of the paper should convey to the reader the precise area covered by the report, but should be as brief as possible. If brevity is genuinely difficult, it is advisable to give a brief title containing the main elements and to follow this with a longer sub-title.

3. A brief outline of the area of the research together with the researcher's preliminary thinking should be given as a means of introducing the area of interest.

203

4. A presentation of literature relevant to the study should be given. This should be presented in such a manner as to lead from peripheral or global literature to more specific work in a funnel-like manner so that the "aims" of the study should come as no surprise to the reader.

5. As we pointed out in Chapter 3, research begins with a perceived difficulty or problem and the report must clearly outline this.

6. Following the "problem formulation" or perceived difficulty there must be a clear statement of the methods used in the study. Sometimes, because of the brevity imposed on the report by an editor, this has to be brief unless some new technique has been used. Good research is, as we pointed out in earlier chapters, not a haphazard process and the reader must be given sufficient information to allow him to know that the approach was well considered and that the study could be replicated. In effect, the method section is really the "design" in past tense.

7. In Chapter 12 we showed how data should be presented and interpreted for the reader, but if communication would be enhanced by the use of visual aids such as histograms or graphs, then these should also be used. Sometimes it is advisable to use brief descriptions with a view to bringing the paper to life and to demonstrate areas which often defy formal definition. We have suggested elsewhere that the findings or results section should confine itself to fact and not to speculation. This section should include all information that could not have been known before the study started.

8. Following the results comes the discussion section in which the findings of the study are related and tentative explanations offered for them both in relation to the authors' experience and to the findings of other related studies. Causal explanations for observed findings must be tentative since, in the social sciences, direct cause and effect links are comparatively rare. A good discussion should lead to statements which are factual and to areas where further research is indicated in the light of the findings.

9. It is conventional and *very* desirable to acknowledge at the beginning or the end of the paper any help given to the author. This may be methodological, advice regarding literature, or help given in facilitating the conduct of the study.

10. At the end of the paper it is necessary to attach a bibliography of all works referred to in the text and these should be laid out in consistent

conventional form. Guidance as to the form references should take is normally supplied by the publisher. There are two recognised methods of referencing. One method is to provide a reference number for each article or book as it is referred to in the text and in the bibliography references are then arranged numerically. More commonly the "Harvard" method is used. With this method the surname of the author and the year of publication is given in the text, e.g. (Philip, McCulloch and Smith, 1975), and in the bibliography the references are listed alphabetically according to the first author's surname. For both systems references in a bibliography should take the following format.

BOOKS

These should be given thus:
Author or editor's surname preceding their initials; year of publication; the title of the book which should be underlined; the edition; the publisher and place of publication; number of volumes if more than one.

ARTICLES

Author of article and date of publication is the same as for books. This is followed by: the title of the paper (*not* underlined) in inverted commas; the title of the journal, underlined; the volume number of the journal; the issue number of the journal; the page numbers. Where appropriate the month of issue should be given.

(The reader should note that when items in typescript are underlined they appear in italics when printed.)

In order to demonstrate the points made in this chapter we now present a published journal article. We have also used this paper to demonstrate the whole of the research process by indicating alongside the text the particular aspect covered.

SOME FACTORS AFFECTING THE PREVALENCE OF STAMMERING*

BY

J. W. McCULLOCH

Medical Research Council, Unit for Research on the Epidemiology of Psychiatric Illness, Department of Psychological Medicine, University of Edinburgh

AND

P. G. FAWCETT

Department of Psychological Medicine, University of Edinburgh

Stammering occurs throughout the civilized world and there has been no lack of theories to account for it. Most theories, and they have been well reviewed by Hahn (1943) and Diehl (1958), assume that there is only one important causative factor whether it be organic or psychological. The organic theories implicate cerebral dominance (Travis, 1931; Orton, 1937) supported by electro-encephalogram findings (Jasper, 1937) and genetic studies (Jameson, 1955). Biochemical investigations including endocrine studies have been unproductive (Hill, 1944). Psychoanalysts (Coriat, 1943) have viewed stammering as a specific form of neurosis attributable to pre-genital libidinal fixation. Despert (1943) and West (1943) suggest that an abnormal maternal attitude is one of the most important causes. Johnson and his associates (1959) consider that physical and hereditary factors are of only minor aetiological

LITERATURE REVIEW (NOTE STYLE OF REFERENCING)

* Reprinted with permission from *Brit. J. prev. soc. Med.* **18**, 146–151 (1964).

significance; they have produced a multi-dimensional theory in which stammering is seen as learned behaviour arising early in life when the neuro-muscular speech patterns are developing. According to Johnson and others (1959), Despert (1943), and West (1943), certain parental characteristics are important in the aetiology of stammering in children. They found that the mothers of stammering children had higher and more strict standards of behaviour for their children and were more dissatisfied with their actual behaviour. The mothers seemed more discontented, more striving, more perfectionistic, and more concerned about what their neighbours thought of them than were the parents of control groups. They demanded higher standards of speech than did other parents. The striving for excellence and the associated feelings of dissatisfaction or failure were found to be more prominent in the mothers than in the fathers of stammering children, the fathers tending to adopt a more conciliatory role.

If psychological factors are important in causing stammering, the prevalence might be expected to vary in different sub-cultures; moreover, any observed differences in prevalence might be related to social and psychological differences between stammerers and their families on the one hand, and non-stammerers and their families on the other. The purpose of the present study is to explore these possibilities.

PROBLEM FORMULATION

Previous clinical observations had been made by the authors on adults referred to the Royal Infirmary of Edinburgh for the treatment of stammering. The stammerers, who were mostly males, developed anxiety and stammered more in situations in which they felt their social status was challenged. They disclosed characteristic attitudes which apparently arose out of particular family relationships. Similar

INSIGHT STIMULAT-ING STUDY

observations had been reported by West (1943), Despert (1943), and Johnson and others (1959). The mothers of the patients were often socially insecure with high social aspirations, over-perfectionistic, and anxious about discipline. These characteristics were clearly displayed in relationships with their children. The fathers generally assumed a more passive role and tended to avoid conflict by acquiescing in the demands of the mothers. We endeavoured to repeat these clinical observations in a whole population survey.

} COMPARATIVE RESEARCH

METHOD

All primary school children in local authority schools in the counties of Moray, Nairn, and Banff were studied. The counties comprise three types of community: fishing towns and villages, other rural areas (generally extremely isolated), and small commercial towns.

} PURPOSIVE SAMPLE

For the purpose of the study, towns with a population exceeding 3,000 where occupations were varied were considered "urban commercial"; towns with populations exceeding 3,000 where the basic industry was fishing were considered "urban fishing"; places with populations less than 3,000 where fishing was the main source of livelihood were considered "rural fishing"; all other areas with populations under 3,000 were considered "rural farming". There was one exception: Kinloss, with a population of under 3,000, has a large RAF station with a population far exceeding that of the village, and was classed as "urban commercial" instead of "rural farming" since the members of the local school population were not really the children of rural dwellers.

} NON-PROBABILITY SAMPLE

The marked cultural differences in these areas have been described in "The Third Statistical Account

} INDICATES SOURCE OF "IN-DEPTH" READING FOR THE INTERESTED READER

S.W.R.—H

of Scotland", vol. 10, "The County of Banff" (Scottish Council of Social Service, 1961).

Progress has been so rapid in the commercial towns that they now differ from the larger Scottish cities and towns in little but size. The fishing towns and villages retain many century-old characteristics and are still greatly influenced by the state of the fishing industry. In the fishing areas kinship bonds are still strong and religion plays a much greater part in both family and community life, particularly in the areas which come under the influence of the "Close" and "Open" Brethren, where severe Calvinistic morality contrasts sharply with standards found elsewhere. Extreme religious groups are required to reject most forms of entertainment and not even to participate in the established political and educational life in the community. In this atmosphere parental control is inevitably stricter, more perfectionistic, and more concerned about neighbourhood values. Social striving is still present and is manifest by the obvious show of acceptable symbols of wealth. "Like the monks of old, they renounce the world and its pleasures, but unlike them they take no vows of poverty" (Robinson, 1945). Religion also plays a much more influential part in the farming areas than in the towns and the evidence of change is not clearly so marked. Despite substantial material advancement many of the rural dwellers are still awkward and self-conscious in the towns.

Mothers in both rural and fishing areas are intensely concerned that their children should better themselves but the possibilities for betterment are limited by a lack of local industry. Consequently, there is a high premium on educational success as a means of achieving advancement. If, as Johnson and others (1959), Despert (1943), and West (1943) suggested, the mothers of stammering children have

HYPOTHETICO-
DEDUCTIVE
REASONING

higher and stricter standards of behaviour and are more striving and more perfectionistic, one would expect to find a higher prevalence of stammering in areas where the general standards of behaviour are more perfectionistic and strict, where children come more closely under the influence of parents because of greatly limited peer-group activities, and where striving for success is restricted by lack of local industry. We believed that this would hold good for the fishing and rural areas of Moray, Nairn, and Banff. We believed also that, by comparing these areas with an urban commercial area where standards are less stringent, where parental influence is lessened by greater peer-group activity, and where there is more available and greater choice of occupation, differences in the prevalence of stammering would be demonstrated and that these differences would be due to the different psychological and social influences to which the children were subjected.

PROBLEM FORMULATION

The study was restricted to primary school children because the literature indicated that stammering normally begins between the ages of 3 and 5 years and often disappears after the age of 11 or 12 years. Secondary schools were not included because they are almost always located in the towns and the teachers know less about the parents and because of the problems involved in obtaining controls from the same area of residence. All information about the families was obtained from the teachers.

SELECTION AND DEFINITION OF THE SAMPLE

With the co-operation of the Directors of Education of HM Inspector of Schools, all head teachers were asked to estimate the amount of speech defect in their respective schools. The replies indicated that there were enough cases and a sufficient variation to justify the study. Class teachers were then asked to complete a questionnaire for each child who stam-

FEASIBILITY STUDY

mered and for the next child of the same sex on the CONTROL GROUP
register who did not stammer, with the following
information; name, address, date of birth, father's
occupation (and, where applicable, his absences
from home for occupational or other reason),
sibship size, position of the child in the sibship,
estimate of the child's personal tidiness. The child's
intelligence, measured or estimated, was given QUESTIONNAIRE CONTENT
together with an account of the mother's attitude to
the child in terms of aspiration and education. Lastly,
teachers were asked to describe the mother's
personality and to make any other comment.

The questionnaire was designed to elicit answers
from the teachers in their educational rather than in
their lay capacities. One question called for a
personality description of the mother, but teachers
supplied information regarding family and inter-
personal relationships without specific questioning.
Though there were differences in the quality of this
information, it was given because the teachers felt
it to be important. They were unaware of our
hypotheses and, indeed, had no contact with us until
after the completion of the questionnaires. The
completed forms were returned to HM Inspector of
Schools, who assigned each pair to its appropriate
area, *i.e.* urban commercial, urban fishing, rural
farming, or rural fishing. Though he was unaware of
our hypotheses, his help had been enlisted, because
of his local knowledge, to define the areas before the
questionnaires were compiled. The questionnaires
were sent to us together with the total number of
pupils in each school.

We then interviewed 85 per cent of the subjects STUDY DESIGN
(Note definition of
cases and inter-
observer reliability)
(stammerers) and controls (next pupil) in order to
verify that the subjects stammered and the controls
did not, to obtain further information about the
children, and to gather as much local knowledge as

possible from teachers and other sources. Any additional subjects discovered were added to this study and all children about whose speech there was some doubt were examined.

We compared our assessments with those of the two speech therapists for the area. With two exceptions our findings tallied, and since there was a discrepancy of less than 2 per cent, between what we called stammering, what the teachers called stammering, and what the speech therapists called stammering we accepted that the remaining 15 per cent of the subjects were stammerers because the therapists agreed with the teachers. The speech therapists and in some cases we ourselves confirmed the absence of stammerers in the schools making nil returns.

The Director of Education for the City of Edinburgh kindly supplied data about the prevalence of stammering in children in local authority schools in the City to permit further cultural comparison.

FINDINGS

The total population of 12,448 primary school children (males 6,428: females 6,020) yielded 102 children who stammered (males 87: females 15; male:female ratio 5.8:1). The distribution by area is shown in Table I.

PREVALENCE BY SEX, AGE, AND AREA

For boys the urban commercial areas have significantly fewer stammerers than all other areas ($\chi^2 = 5.446$; P < 0.02; 1 d/f).

The Figure shows that the prevalence of stammering rises with age in both the northern population and in Edinburgh.

The prevalence rate does not vary with the size of the school for schools with fifty or more pupils, but

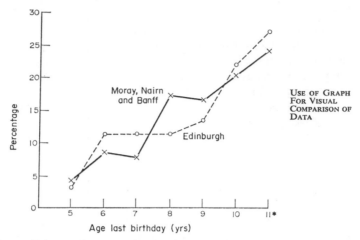

USE OF GRAPH
FOR VISUAL
COMPARISON OF
DATA

FIGURE.—Point prevalence rate of stammering amongst primary school children, 1963.
* A very few children included here in both numerator and denominator had passed their 12th birthday.

schools with fewer than fifty pupils yielded twice the rate for all schools. This difference is highly significant (Table II) and persists even when urban schools are excluded (Table III).

We did not know about school size until the data were in our possession, but we feel that it helps to demonstrate the higher prevalence rates in rural areas since schools with fewer than fifty pupils typify remote areas. It also demonstrates that closer supervision in academic spheres may also be a factor to be considered in that teacher/pupil relationships in small schools tends to be much more personal.

INTELLIGENCE

In our study stammerers have a lower I.Q. than controls (using Kendall's non-parametric test of trend (Table IV) $\tau = -0.23$; $P = 0.0009$). No I.Q.s were available for the stammerers in the

TABLE I. DISTRIBUTION BY AREA AND SEX

Area		Males			Females		
		No. of Pupils	No. of Stammerers	Rate per 1,000	No. of Pupils	No. of Stammerers	Rate per 1,000
Urban	Fishing	1,122	19	16.9	1,080	1	0.9
	Commercial	2,398	22	9.2	2,166	3	1.4
Rural	Fishing	652	10	15.3	688	4	5.8
	Farming	2 256	36	16.0	2,086	7	3.4
Total ..	.. ..	6,428	87	13.5	6,020	15	2.5

QUANTITATIVE DATA

TABLE II. SCHOOL SIZE—ALL SIZES

No. on School Roll	No. of Schools	No. of Pupils at Risk	No. of Stammerers	Prevalence per 1,000
< 50	40	1,147	21	18
50 —	21	1,343	11	8
100 —	7	871	10	11
150 —	7	1,188	12	10
200 +	19	7,899	48	6
Total	94	12,448	102	8

χ^2 Schools < 50 × All Others = 15.904; P < 0.001; 1 d/f.

TABLE III. SCHOOL SIZE IN RURAL AND FISHING AREAS

No. on School Roll	No. of Schools	No. of Pupils at Risk	No. of Stammerers	Prevalence per 1,000
< 50	40	1,147	21	18
50 —	20	1,268	11	9
100 —	6	760	8	10
150 —	7	1,188	12	10
200 +	9	3,521	25	7
Total	82	7,884	77	10

χ^2 Schools < 50 × All Others = 10.127; P < 0.002; 1 d/f.

TABULAR DATA PRESENTATION USING BIVARIATE TABLES AND SHOWING RESULTS OF STATISTICAL ANALYSIS (CHI-SQUARE TEST)

Edinburgh schools, so that no comparison with the trend found in the north was possible. However, for Edinburgh, a comparison between normal schools and schools for the mentally handicapped shows a highly significant greater prevalence of stammering in the latter (χ^2 = 32.62; P = < 0.00001; 1 d/f).

Again, using Kendall's test of trend, there was no significant differences in intelligence between pupils (whether stammerers or controls) in urban commercial and other areas.

FAMILY SOCIAL PATTERNS (Table V)

(i) *High Aspiring Mother.*—When compared with mothers of controls a significantly greater number of

TABLE IV. INTELLIGENCE OF STAMMERERS AND CONTROLS

Children	Area	Above Average I.Q. > 110		Average I.Q. 90–109		Below Average I.Q. < 90	
Stammerers	Urban Commercial	1	} 9	14	} 50	9	} 29
	Rural and Fishing	8		36		20	
Controls	Urban Commercial	4	} 12	19	} 67	1	} 9
	Rural and Fishing	8		48		8	

TABLE V. SOCIAL PATTERNS

Social Criteria	Stammerers per cent ($n = 102$)	Controls per cent ($n = 89$)	Significance of Difference (P)
(i) High-Aspiring Mother	58	11	< 0.0001
(ii) Extreme Personal Neatness	44	27	< 0.02
(iii) Social Disorganisation in Family	30	9	< 0.0003

the mothers of stammerers had higher than average aspirations for their children.

(*ii*) *Child's Personal Neatness.*—A significantly greater number of the stammerers were above average in their personal neatness.

(*iii*) *Social Disorganization*—There was a significantly higher incidence of social disorganization in the homes of the subjects than in the homes of the controls. In this context social disorganization was evidenced by such factors as financial difficulties, marital problems, and strained inter-personal relations, with, in some cases ill-treatment of children. Many children from socially-disorganized homes had parents who were mentally ill, mentally subnormal, or markedly mentally unstable. All information referred to in this section was given in response to the question "any other comment". Because, in the field of psychological disorders, the teachers were lay observers, no qualification was

CONFIRMATION OF USE OF INSIGHT-STIMULATING EXAMPLES

UNEXPECTED FINDINGS

possible. We therefore confined ourselves to using their descriptive terms.

Examples of teachers' reports indicating social disorganization were:

> "Mother has a low I.Q. Unstable. A bad manager."
> "Unstable mother. Spoils child badly materially with great emotional neglect."
> "Illegitimate child but mother later married then divorced. Remarried but now separated and awaiting second divorce."
> "This child is in the care of the Local Authority because of parental cruelty."
> "Mother attempts to cope with four small children in a small caravan and has to 'punish' them continually. Not a well-integrated personality and clearly finds it hard to manage her children."

QUALITATIVE DESCRIPTIVE DATA

Of the children from socially-disorganized families, 36 per cent had I.Q.s lower than average compared with 33 per cent of the total sample. 29 per cent of the stammerers with I.Q.s of average or above came from socially-disorganized families. Ten stammerers who had mothers below average in aspirations and six stammerers who were below average in neatness came from socially-disorganized families yet did not have low I.Q.s. Social disorganization, therefore, seems to play a part in the genesis of stammering independently of low I.Q.

FAMILIAL OCCURRENCE.—Although this information was not sought specifically, a history of stammering in the immediate family was reported in 24 cases involving nineteen families. In each of the three sets of twins (ovularity uncertain) in the survey, only one child stammered.

Intensity of the Stammer.—The girls who stammered were without exception more seriously afflicted than the boys. We did not find any significant factors to account for this finding; social disorganization, however, was reported more often for girls (40 per cent) than for boys (29 per cent).

Miscellaneous.—There were no differences between the subjects and controls in respect of sibship size or ordinal position in the sibship. The fathers of subjects were somewhat, but not significantly, more often absent from home than fathers of controls.

A specific precipitating event was reported in 11 per cent of the cases.

DISCUSSION

Morganstern (1953) found that the prevalence of stammering per 1,000 in the primary schools of Edinburgh was 21.2 for males and 3.6 for females (Table VIa). Since our own Edinburgh findings were five times lower, we studied his method in detail to attempt to account for the discrepancy. His rates appeared to be derived only from observations of children in the oldest primary school age group of Edinburgh local authority schools. Since, as we have shown (Figure), this age group contains the highest number of stammerers both in the north and in Edinburgh, we have reason to believe that there were errors in the numerator and denominator of his prevalence equation which both acted to produce an excessive rate.

FAULTY LOGIC OF INFERENCE—NOTE THE NECESSITY OF CRITICAL EVALUATION OF PUBLISHED WORK

TABLE VIa. STAMMERING PREVALENCE RATES PER 1,000 FOR PRIMARY SCHOOLS

Area		Sex			Males per 100 Fe- males
		Males	Fe- males	Both Sexes	
Moray, Nairn, and Banff	Urban Fishing	16.9	0.9	9.1	1,820
	Urban Commercial	9.2	1.4	5.5	664
	Rural Fishing	15.3	5.8	10.5	264
	Rural Farming	16.0	3.4	9.9	475
Edinburgh	1962/63 Data	4.0	1.0	2.5	391
	Morganstern (1953)	21.2	3.6	12.5	588

We then projected his rates for the oldest age group onto the whole Edinburgh school primary population at that time, using as a basis the age distribution of stammerers in Edinburgh which we obtained. The resultant corrected prevalence rates (Table VIb) are similar to those we found in the urban commercial areas in Moray, Nairn, and Banff. The projection from Morganstern's data yields a rather higher prevalence rate for Edinburgh than our 1962–63 figures (Table VIa), but when he supplied us with the number of stammerers for this year the Director of Education indicated that a number of the less severe cases were not included by the speech therapists who compiled the data.

TABLE VIb. COMPARISON OF PREVALENCE RATES OF PRESENT STUDY WITH THOSE OF MORGANSTERN (1953)

Area	Sex			Males per 100 Females
	Males	Females	Both Sexe	
Moray, Nairn and Banff Urban Commercial	9.2	1.4	5.5	664
Morganstern (1953) adjusted to Edinburgh 1962–63 Age Distributions	9.6	1.7	5.7	570

The prevalence of stammering in the rural and fishing districts is clearly higher than in the urban commercial areas. We can find no evidence of a hereditary or a physical factor (such as a high incidence of minimal birth injury) peculiar to these areas to account for it. Although there is an association between stammering and low intelligence, we have found no positive association between low intelligence and rural school populations as a whole, nor have we been able to demonstrate any relationship between intelligence and area of residence in either stammerers or non-stammerers. The positive

LOGIC OF INFERENCE

relationship between stammering and low intelligence cannot therefore account for the higher prevalence in the rural and fishing areas.

It seems most likely that family and cultural differences explains our findings, although conceivably there may be a genetically-conditioned predisposition towards stammering which is activated by environmental influences. Our findings support the findings of Johnson and others (1959). Despert (1943), and West (1943) regarding the prevalence among stammerers of high aspiring mothers and of personal neatness (Table V). There are also cultural peculiarities in the fishing and rural areas which may be responsible for the greater prevalence of stammering. In small rural schools with small classes, which we have shown to be associated with a high prevalence of stammering, teachers are able to give more individual attention to educational and speech development. One aim is to reduce the broad local dialects. Perhaps, therefore, in the rural areas, an educational process rather than the family exerts a particular influence on the child's speech. We have suggested that a particular parental influence might be related to the prevailing religion. This influence might be expected to be stronger in view of these children's relative isolation from wider social contacts. In the more remote areas teachers reported that many of their pupils were virtually isolated in the lonely farms and crofts, and older children were often expected to help on the farm so that peer-group activities were restricted even further. Therefore, if parental influences are important factors in the aetiology of stammering, they would be expected to be greater in isolated communities. Some confirmation of this hypothesis emerged in our interviews with the children, when we found that in the rural schools the boys tended to give their father's

LOGIC OF INFERENCE

occupation as their own occupation of choice for
the future, whereas in the urban commercial areas
their choice of occupation was more varied and
imaginative.

Our data provide support for the view that social
and psychological factors play a role in the production
of stammering and that these factors may be related
to relatively strict methods of upbringing associated
with anxiety and high parental aspiration. This
finding is in agreement with that of Johnson and his
associates (1959). We have shown, however, that a
significant group of stammerers came from socially
disorganized homes and families. These families
were characterized by social stress, anxiety, and overt
conflict unlike the apparently well-integrated families
described by Johnson.

All the social variables set out in Table V were
considered by area and the distribution for each
showed no significant differences. For the stammerers
there was a slight tendency for social disorganization
to occur more frequently in the urban commercial
area, so that this factor cannot be held to account for
the higher prevalence in the rural and fishing
districts. Using the control group to make comparison between the areas for each of the social
variables did not demonstrate any significant differences, but the numbers were rather small for
statistical treatment. In our findings low intelligence
and social disorganization were not significantly
related and may operate independently (Table V).

SUMMARY

The prevalence of stammering in all primary
school children in the counties of Moray, Nairn, and
Banff and in the city of Edinburgh is presented.

Personal and social data about stammerers and

non-stammerers have been compared. The prevalence of stammering increased with age. The male:female ratio among stammerers varied in the different areas from 2.6 : 1 to 18.2 : 1. Stammering was found to be significantly more prevalent in fishing and rural farming areas than in the urban commercial areas. Stammerers had lower I.Q.s than controls, but there was no relationship between intelligence and area of residence. Mothers of stammering children had higher social aspirations than had mothers of controls. Stammerers were neater in their personal appearance and were more likely to come from socially-disorganized families. There were no differences in family size or sibship position. Fathers of stammerers lived apart from the family somewhat more often than fathers of controls. The bearing of these findings upon the aetiology of stammering is discussed.

We are indebted to Mr John J. Reid, HM Inspector of Schools, for his advice and practical help in organising this study. Miss Gray, Speech Therapist for Banffshire, and Miss Fletcher, Speech Therapist for Moray and Nairn, gave valuable assistance in the ascertainment of stammering in their respective areas and we are grateful to them. We should also like to express our thanks to Mr W. F. Lindsay, Director of Education for Moray and Nairn, and Mr James McNaught, Director of Education for Banffshire, and all the teachers in both areas without whose co-operation the study would not have been possible.

ACKNOWLEDGE-MENTS

REFERENCES

Coriat, I. H. (1943). *Nerv. Child.* **2**, 167.
Despert, J. L. (1943). *Amer. J. Orthopyschiat.*, **13**, 517.
Diehl, C. F. (1958). "A Compendium of Research and Theory on Stuttering." Thomas, Springfield, Ill.
Hahn, E. F. (1943). "Stuttering: Significant Theories and Therapies." Stanford University Press, California.
Hill, H. (1944). *J. Speech Dis.* **9**, 245; 289.
Jameson, A. M. (1955). *Speech*, **19**, 60.
Jasper, H. H. (1937). *Psychol. Bull.* **34**, 411.

"HARVARD" STYLE OF BIBLIOGRAPHY (MODIFIED BY THE "HOUSE STYLE" OF THE JOURNAL, I.E. NO TITLES FOR JOURNAL ARTICLES, NO ISSUE NUMBER AND ONLY 1ST PAGE OF ARTICLES GIVEN)

Johnson, W., and Associates (1959). "The Onset of Stuttering,"
    University of Minnesota Press, Minniapolis.
Morganstern, J. J. (1953). "Psychological and Social Factors
    in Children's Stammering." Ph.D. Thesis, Edinburgh.
Orton, S. T. (1937). "Reading, Writing and Speech Problems
    in Children." Norton, New York.
Robinson, W. (1945). "The Shattered Cross." Berean Press,
    Birmingham.
Scottish Council of Social Service (1961). "Third Statistical
    Account of Scotland", vol. 10. "The County of Banff",
    ed. H. Hamilton for The University of Aberdeen,
    chapters 2, 4, 6, 8. Collins, Glasgow.
Travis, L. E. (1931). "Speech Pathology", Appleton, New York.
West, R. (1943). *Nerv. Child*, **2,** 96.

In many instances a report may be written at the point when a particular part of a large piece of research or one of a series of interconnected research projects have been completed. However, for smaller studies it may mark the completion of the whole project. In either case the foregoing points relating to presentation and write-up of the report still apply, except that an indication would be made if the reported study was one of a series or part of a larger work.

Although the report may well seem to be the final stage of the research process, it also marks the beginning, since it should stimulate the researcher and others to continue to expand the particular field of knowledge. The very act of writing the report is also the point at which the researcher himself may develop insights into the short-comings of his own work, and establish the logical sequence of steps which should inevitably follow on from the completed work.

Good research serves no useful purpose if it is not utilised. We would therefore draw the reader's attention to the need to be able to evaluate critically a research report either during the process of his own research or as a consumer who wishes to enhance his practice. It must be emphasised that not all research is good research and that both the producer and the consumer must be able to distinguish the good from the bad. It follows therefore that both must understand how research findings should be presented and the value of critical "in-depth" reading.

Research is not finite, but a continually expanding and refining process moving in small methodical steps; this is discussed more fully in the concluding chapter.

Conclusions

IN the preceding chapter we have attempted to spell out in considerable detail the "why" as well as the "how" of research. The "how" involves knowing how to formulate problems, how to set up appropriate research designs, how to use statistical procedures which can clarify findings and how to report these activities in a meaningful way. The "why" is concerned with the wider issues of verifying what we think we know and with expanding professional knowledge by integrating empirical findings with existing conceptual formulations. Statistics and data-gathering are a very useful part of the process of increasing knowledge, but we must re-emphasise that they are *aids* to understanding and communicating. If we have no ideas about our chosen field, we are not likely to discover anything interesting, because even if our data collection and analysis are done strictly by the book, the interpretation and integration with existing knowledge must be a human, subjective affair.

In interpreting and communicating research we are forced to use language which can be understood by all. The words we normally use are very imprecise and part of the whole research process is to provide more meaningful labels which convey their information with precision. In many instances the labels we use are of an either/or nature. For example, we talk of "client" or "non-client" as though there were no similarities between the two and that they were therefore mutually exclusive. Because of this it is tempting to look for characteristics which determine the label instead of looking for similarities between clients and non-clients which might enhance our understanding of the former. Having applied a label to an individual we attribute to that individual *all* the characteristics surrounding that label. Consider the well-established correlation between the incidence of overcrowding and that of delinquency. This association does not permit us to assume that all people reared in overcrowded conditions are liable to become delinquent, nor that *all* delinquents come from overcrowded conditions. The pertinent questions to be asked on finding such correlations are not only why the two variables are related but also why, on the one hand, some youngsters from overcrowded homes do not become delinquent, and on the other, some delinquents come from homes which are not overcrowded. It is also important to establish the meaning of the terms "overcrowding" and "delinquency"; it could be that by changing our definition of delinquency to include or exclude certain factors then the correlation might change. We have shown, in Chapter 11 and elsewhere, how some of these refinements might be achieved by considering research results in their proper context—how they relate to the existing body of knowledge in any particular area. Here again statistics can be seen as an aid to thinking.

Researchers are aware of the need to keep abreast of the literature because they need to relate their results and thinking with the work of others. It is just as necessary for the non-researcher to keep abreast of the literature so that he can integrate new findings with his own awareness and knowledge of the field. For both kinds of individual, discrepant findings should act as a stimulus for further investigation. Our book is intended to encourage the reader to behave in this way, but by its very introductory nature the reader will find it necessary to go further in some or all areas as his sophistication grows. With this in mind we have listed at the end of this chapter a number of books which can be consulted as the need arises. All practitioners meet with problems which they cannot explain; light can be shed on these perceived difficulties either by searching for other people's approaches to them or by personally investigating the area. Hopefully, our book will facilitate both these approaches.

Recommended Reference Reading

GUILFORD, J. P. (1965) *Fundamental Statistics in Psychology and Education.* New York: McGraw-Hill.

HARMAN, H. H. (1967) *Modern Factor Analysis.* Chicago: University of Chicago Press.

OPPENHEIM, A. N. (1966) *Questionnaire Design and Attitude Measurement.* London: Heinemann.

POLANSKY, N. A. (Ed.) (1960) *Social Work Research.* Chicago: University of Chicago Press.

SELLTIZ, C., JAHODA, M., DEUTSCH, M. and COOK, S. W. (1959) *Research Methods in Social Relations.* New York: Holt.

Index

Index

231

Feasibility of research *see* Research
Findings (*see also* Research)
  action on 77
  chance 77
'F' ratio 123, 124
Frequency tables 86

Gaussian *see* Normal distribution
Graphs, use of 87 ff

Hierarchical syndrome analysis 153 ff
Histograms, use of 86, 87
Hostility and direction of hostility
  questionnaire (H.D.H.Q.) 184
Hypotheses 23, 26
  examples of 26, 29, 30
  null form of 26, 83, 113

Inference, logic of 44, 75, 83, 220 ff,
  225 ff
  example of 210
  faulty, example of 219
Instruments, data collection
  categorisation of 15 ff
  measuring accuracy of 15
  types of 19, 36 ff
Interpretation of research findings
  225 ff
Interval scales 20
Intervening variables 26
Interviewing 40 ff
  conduct in 41
  guide to 41
  probing and prompting in 41
  recording 41

Kendall's rank order coefficient of
  correlation (tau) 131 ff
  coefficient of 131
  contingency tables in formula for,
    135 ff, 136 ff
  formula for 132 ff
  statistical significance, formula for
    134, 135

Latent root 172, 177 ff
Literature
  abstracts 69 ff
    education 71
    general 70
    law and criminology 71
    psychology 71
    social work 70
    sociology 70
  bibliographies
    of bibliographies 55 ff
    general 48 ff
    in reports 204, 205
  catalogues 48 ff
  conferences and symposia 59 ff
  dictionaries 56 ff
  directories 66
  encyclopaedias 56 ff
  government publications 62 ff
  guides to research 53 ff
  handbooks 58
  periodicals 67 ff
  presentation of 204
    example of 207 ff
  psychology 47 ff
  referring, forms of 205
  reviews 55 ff
    example of 209
  searching 25, 72 ff
    continuing need for 226
  social, guides to 47 ff
  sources of 47 ff
  statistical information 63 ff

Matrices 143 ff, 165 ff
  factor 170, 173, 178
  factor loading 172 ff
    Harman's formula for significance
      181 ff
    orthogonality of 174
  reduced factor 170, 178, 181
Means *see* Central tendency, measures of
  and Statistics, tests in
Median *see* Central tendency, measures
  of *and* Statistics, tests in
Measurements
  accuracy of 15
  definition of 19